NABOKOV'S

INVITATION

TO A BEHEADING

A Critical Companion

NABOKOV'S

INVITATION

TO A BEHEADING

A Critical Companion

Edited by Julian W. Connolly

Northwestern University Press

The American Association of Teachers of

Slavic and East European Languages

Northwestern University Press

Evanston, Illinois 60208-4210

ISBN 0-8101-1271-X

Library of Congress Cataloging-in-Publication Data

Nabokov's Invitation to a beheading : a critical companion / edited by Julian W.
Connolly.

p.   cm — (Northwestern/AATSEEL critical companions to Russian literature)

Includes bibliographical references.

ISBN 0-8101-1271-X (pbk. : alk. paper)

1. Nabokov, Vladimir Vladimirovich, 1899–1977. Priglashenie na
kazn'. I. Connolly, Julian W. II. Series.

PG3476.N3P7335   1997

891.73'42—dc21   97-23097

                                                               CIP

Contents

DBJ

Acknowledgments

I would like to thank the following individuals and organizations for their help in the production of this volume: The Modern Language Association of America, for permission to reprint Dale Peterson's article, "Nabokov's *Invitation*: Literature as Execution," which originally appeared in *PMLA* 96 (1981): 824–36 (Copyright © 1981 by The Modern Language Association of America); Robert Alter, for permission to reprint his article, "*Invitation to a Beheading*: Nabokov and the Art of Politics," which first appeared in *TriQuarterly* 17 (1970): 41–59; Vladimir Alexandrov and D. Barton Johnson, for their willingness to rework and revise earlier studies of *Invitation to a Beheading* for this volume; Brian Boyd, who collected and annotated the source material related to the genesis of *Priglashenie na kazn'* and its subsequent literary transformations; and Dmitri Nabokov, who gave his permission to publish excerpts from his parents' correspondence (Copyright © 1996 by the Article 3 b Trust under the Will of Vladimir Nabokov). I also would like to express my appreciation to Barry Scherr, who initially encouraged me to take on this project. Finally, I owe a special debt of gratitude to my family – Sandra, William, and Thomas – for their boundless support and good cheer.

A Note on Transliteration

I have followed the recommendations outlined by J. Thomas Shaw in his *The Transliteration of Modern Russian for English-Language Publications* (Madison: University of Wisconsin Press, 1967). In bibliographic citations and in the transliteration of Russian words I have used the Library of Congress transliteration system with the diacritical marks omitted (Shaw's System II). In the main body of the text I have made further modications (see Shaw's System I) to render Russian names in forms that may be more familiar to an English-speaking audience (e.g., *Andrey* for *Andrei*).

I  INTRODUCTION

Invitation to a Beheading: Nabokov's "Violin in a Void"

JULIAN W. CONNOLLY

We should always remember that the work of art is invariably the creation of a new world, so that the first thing we should do is to study that new world as closely as possible, approaching it as something brand new, having no obvious connection with the worlds we already know. When this new world has been closely studied, then and only then let us examine its links with other worlds, other branches of knowledge.
—Vladimir Nabokov, "Good Readers and Good Writers"

More than thirty years after writing *Invitation to a Beheading* (*Priglashenie na kazn'*), Vladimir Nabokov told an interviewer that this work was his "dreamiest and most poetical novel," and that of all his novels he felt the "greatest esteem" for it.[1] Initially drafted "in one fortnight of wonderful excitement and sustained inspiration" (*SO*, 68) during the summer of 1934, *Invitation to a Beheading* was certainly the most unusual of the eight novels he had written up to this point in his career.[2] The work focuses on the impressions of a man sentenced to death for the mysterious crime of "gnostical turpitude," a crime so terrible in the eyes of the other characters that they must refer to it through such circumlocutions as "impenetrability," "opacity," and "occlusion."[3] On closer inspection, however, it appears that the essential crime for which this man has been condemned is that he is *different* from those around him. In his words, he is the only one among them who is truly "alive" (52/62). The resulting conflict between the protagonist, Cincinnatus C., and his jailers has engaged and intrigued readers ever since the novel first appeared in the émigré journal *Sovremennye zapiski* in 1935–36.[4]

Upon opening this book, the reader steps into a strange, even bizarre world. In the novel's first lines, the death sentence is announced to Cincinnatus, and all in the courtroom rise, "exchanging smiles" (11/25). This sense of satisfaction or pleasure at the announcement of a death sentence may seem out of place, but the peculiarity of that moment pales before a scene that soon follows – the entrance of the prison director into Cincinnatus's cell. The scene begins with a description of the entering figure:

> He was dressed as always in a frock coat and held himself exquisitely straight, chest out, one hand in his bosom the other behind his back. A perfect toupee, black as pitch, and with a waxy parting, smoothly covered his head. His face, selected without love, with its thick sallow cheeks and somewhat obsolete system of wrinkles, was enlivened in a sense by two, and only by two, bulging eyes. Moving his legs evenly in his columnar trousers, he strode from the wall to the table, almost to the cot – but in spite of his majestic solidity, he calmly vanished, dissolving into the air. A minute later, however, the door opened once again, this time with the familiar grating sound, and dressed as always in a frock coat, his chest out, in came the same person. (14–15/28)

Not only are the director's movements perplexing (he enters the room, dissolves, and then reenters), but the narrator's handling of descriptive detail is also puzzling. When the narrator notes that the director's face was enlivened "by two, *and only by two*, bulging eyes" [emphasis added], the reader wonders: why "only" by two? Does the narrator think there should be more? And in what sense is the director's face "selected without love"? Selected by whom?

Having been exposed to such an odd scene, the reader soon encounters further puzzles. In chapter 2, the narrator describes Cincinnatus dragging a table in his cell over to a wall in which a window is set high above him. Cincinnatus climbs onto a chair on the table and tries without success to look out the window. He is apprehended there by his jailer, Rodion, who lifts him down from the table and moves the table back to its original position (28–29/40–42). On the very next page, however, the narrator again describes Cincinnatus attempting to move the table, but this time the narrator notes: "alas, the legs had been bolted down for ages" (30/42). One might be tempted to interpret the first scene in which Cincinnatus moved the table as a kind of fantasy or dream on Cincinnatus's part, but the jailer later recounts this very scene to Cincinnatus's lawyer (40/51). Thus the reader is left with two contradictory impressions, and the narrator makes no attempt to reconcile or explain the disparity.

What kind of world *is* this? What are Nabokov's readers meant to make of the material presented to them? The critical responses to the work have been numerous and varied, and a brief survey of these responses would be useful.

The Critical Response to *Invitation to a Beheading*

The earliest reviewers of the novel (those who commented on it as it was being published serially in *Sovremennye zapiski*) were understandably hesitant to make definitive evaluations.[5] They took note of the peculiarities of Nabokov's vision, but they generally preferred to withold judgment until they had seen the finished product. Some readers, however, expressed consternation at what they found in the novel. One critic wrote: "The first and most sincere reaction after reading through *Invitation to a Beheading* is perplexity. What is this? Why was this book written? Perplexity and bitterness come over the reader. It's clear that Sirin [Nabokov's pen name—Ed.] is seeking new paths. But it is no less clear that he has wandered into a blind alley. . . . An inexorable book, a terrifying and tormented book."[6]

Over time, however, a series of cogent and coherent interpretations of the novel emerged, each one accenting some aspect of Nabokov's vision. Perhaps the most straightforward line of interpretation concentrated on the plight of the individual persecuted by a collective that uses force to coerce its members into conformity. Such interpreters, of course, were mindful of the totalitarian regimes that ruled the Soviet Union and Germany at the time the novel was written. The émigré critic Vladimir Varshavsky, for example, viewed

Cincinnatus as an "internal émigré" who refuses to follow the "general line" and therefore has been condemned to death.[7] More recently, David Rampton has analyzed the political and sociohistorical implications raised in Nabokov's treatment of Cincinnatus and his world in the novel.[8] Viewed from this perspective, *Invitation to a Beheading* has been read as a variant of the literary genre known as *dystopia*, a type of anti-utopia which, as Gary Saul Morson puts it, "discredits utopias by portraying the likely effects of their realization."[9] Indeed, *Invitation to a Beheading* has been linked with such works as Yevgeny Zamyatin's novel *We* and George Orwell's *1984*.[10]

In his foreword to the English translation of *Invitation to a Beheading* Nabokov himself commented on the historical context within which the novel was composed ("some fifteen years after escaping from the Bolshevist regime, and just before the Nazi regime reached its full volume of welcome" [5]), yet he did so in order to dismiss this as a relevant issue: "The question whether or not my seeing both [regimes—Ed.] in terms of one dull beastly farce had any effect on this book, should concern the good reader as little as it does me" (5). He then went on to disparage any comparison of his work with that of Orwell or "other popular purveyors of illustrated ideas and publicistic fiction" (6).

Why did Nabokov resist so strenuously any reading of the novel that might consider it in light of the political experience of twentieth-century totalitarianism or of dystopian fiction such as Orwell's? Such a stance is characteristic for Nabokov, and he often used the forewords or prefaces to the English translations of his Russian novels to discourage ideological analyses of his work.[11] His concerns are dual. In the first place, he was a staunch defender of the principle of individuality in art, and he opposed any reading that would have the effect of minimizing the unique traits of a work by regarding it as a member of a general class or category. In fact, to categorize *Invitation to a Beheading* in terms of a larger class would be to subject the novel to the same kind of reductive treatment accorded Cincinnatus by the conformist beings who surround him.[12]

What is more, a reading that concentrates on the sociopolitical dimensions of the work might leave *other* aspects of the work (its narrative technique, descriptive imagery, humor, etc.) unnoticed or insufficiently appreciated. The polychromatic blaze of Nabokov's art would be reduced to a somber, monochromatic plane. When Nabokov declares "I have no social purpose, no moral message; I've no general ideas to exploit" (*SO*, 16), he is attempting to carve out for his work a space free from heavy-handed ideological readings, readings that are bound by time and place. As he puts it, "[T]here can be no question that what makes a work of fiction safe from larvae and rust is not its social importance but its art, only its art" (*SO*, 33).[13]

Nabokov's own insistence that a literary work be judged solely in terms of its *art* points to a second interpretive approach to *Invitation to a Beheading*, one that focuses on the *aesthetic* implications of the novel. Nabokov's fellow émigré poet, Vladislav Khodasevich (whom Nabokov called "the greatest Russian poet of our time" [see *SO*, 223]) is often credited with drawing attention to the primacy of art as a theme in Nabokov's work. In an influential article written in 1937, Khodasevich affirmed: "The life of the artist and the life of a device in the consciousness of the artist – this is Sirin's theme, revealing itself to some degree or other in almost every one of his writings, beginning with *The Defense*."[14] From Khodasevich's perspective, the strange machinations depicted in *Invitation to a Beheading* are merely "the play of the stage-hand elves, the play of devices and images that fill the consciousness or, rather, the creative delirium of Cincinnatus"; the ending of the novel depicts "the return of the artist from creative work to reality" ("On Sirin," 98). This line of investigation has been followed up by a number of insightful readings, including sensitive discussions by Ellen Pifer and Leona Toker.[15] In his eloquent essay "*Invitation to a Beheading*: Nabokov and the Art of Politics" (included in the present volume), Robert Alter illustrates how the aesthetic and the sociopolitical dimensions of the novel are interwoven in the novel: the resulting synthesis provides a compelling view of the way totalitarian regimes inevitably debase and disfigure authentic art.

The present volume also contains an essay that offers an ingenious variation on a metaliterary reading of the novel. In "Nabokov's *Invitation*: Literature as Execution," Dale Peterson considers Cincinnatus not so much as a beleaguered artist as a beleaguered literary *character*; that is, when Cincinnatus triumphantly emerges from the oppressive constraints of the society that has imprisoned him, Peterson argues that Cincinnatus is not only escaping from a world of fictional beings who wish to behead him, he is also escaping from the predatory attention of the novel's *readers*, who wish to take him apart and fathom his enigmatic depths for their own satisfaction.

A third major line of interpretation for Nabokov's novel moves beyond the political and aesthetic to a broader metaphysical plane. A number of critics, including Julian Moynahan, Robert Grossmith, and Sergej Davydov, have taken up the challenge of investigating Cincinnatus's supposed crime of "gnostical turpitude" and have examined Nabokov's extensive use of Gnostic motifs and symbolic systems in the novel.[16] While Grossmith and Davydov have provided the most detailed description of Gnostic elements in *Invitation to a Beheading*, Vladimir Alexandrov offers a broader reading of the novel's metaphysical dimensions; he argues that a metaphysical vision both undergirds and is expressed through the aesthetic and ideological elements in the novel (see Alexandrov's article, "The Otherworld in *Invitation to a Beheading*," in the present volume).

When one reads the above-mentioned studies in conjunction with the novel to which they are devoted, one begins to appreciate the complexity and richness of the author's achievement in *Invitation to a Beheading*. As Leona Toker notes, "[E]thics, aesthetics, and metaphysics shade into one another . . . borderlines between them do not exist."[17] To apprehend with greater clarity the richly textured "new world" of Nabokov's novel, we should focus on some of the individual motifs and thematic patterns out of which this world is constructed.

Central Images, Patterns, and Themes

Nabokov's novels consistently feature elaborate patterns of suggestive detail whose overall impact may not be evident until one has arrived at the end of the work. It is only then that one can look back at the novel and discern the delicate tracings that come together to form a meaningful design. This effect bears out Nabokov's conviction that "one cannot *read* a book: one can only reread it."[18] In reading, Nabokov insists, "one should notice and fondle details."[19] In the following sections we shall examine some of the most significant details and thematic patterns embedded in the novel.

THEATRICALITY: EXECUTION AS SPECTACLE

One of the most striking attributes about the society that has imprisoned Cincinnatus in *Invitation to a Beheading* is its *theatricality*. Characters wear costumes and stage makeup; the jailer breaks into song in "the imitation jaunty pose of operatic rakes in the tavern scene" (29/42); the prison director and the executioner consult scripts as they read their speeches; and numerous events in the outside world seem to occur as if they were staged: "A summer thunderstorm, simply yet tastefully *staged*, was *performed* outside" (129/130; emphasis added); "muffled up bats, hanging like wrinkled fruit, *awaited their cue*" (164/163; emphasis added).[20]

This atmosphere of theatricality gradually intensifies as events build toward the ultimate "performance" to be staged in the novel, the public execution of Cincinnatus in "Thriller Square." After the deputy city director makes a series of announcements from the execution platform ("I also remind you that tonight, there will be given with sensational success the new comic opera *Socrates Must Decrease*" [220/215]), the executioner M'sieur Pierre begins to give instructions as if to a lighting director behind the scenes: "Good. Let's begin. The light is a bit harsh . . . Perhaps you could . . . There, that's fine. Thank you. Perhaps just a wee bit more . . . Excellent!" (221/216).

Nabokov's reasons for stressing the theatricality of this world are several. To begin with, this theatricality underscores the sham, derivative nature of the beings who inhabit this space. Unlike Cincinnatus, who possesses a spark of genuine originality, the creatures who surround him have no life of their own: they are like inanimate puppets given a semblance of life by an unseen puppeteer. Moreover, Nabokov wants to confront his readers with an essential (and grotesque) disparity: a man is about to be *murdered*, but those who seek to murder him are looking forward to the event as if it were a *circus spectacle*! Indeed, Pierre notes that "[c]ircus subscription stubs will be honored" for admission to the "performance" (176/174). Nabokov's irony becomes particularly trenchant when he describes how one family sends their child off to watch the execution: "[A] youth came out, and his entire family followed to see him off – this day he had reached *execution-attending age*; mother was smiling through her tears, granny was thrusting a sandwich into his knapsack, kid brother was handing him his staff" (217/212; emphasis added). A conventional genre scene takes on startling new meaning because of the bizarre context in which it appears.

Yet Nabokov's vision here is not entirely fantastic. In his autobiography, *Speak, Memory*, he recalls providing editorial assistance to a young man in Germany whose hobby was attending executions.[21] Later he would utilize the theme again in *Lolita*, when Clare Quilty attempts to stave off his own execution by promising to arrange for Humbert Humbert to "attend executions."[22] Of particular significance for *Invitation to a Beheading*, however, is that this penchant for theatricalizing an execution scene is not simply a personal idiosyncracy, but it is characteristic of Cincinnatus's society as a whole. The grim charade of cooperation between victim and executioner had an eerie counterpart in the so-called show trials that were being held in Russia during the very decade in which this novel was written.[23]

MASKS AND DISGUISES

A second aspect of the theatrical dimension of Cincinnatus's world is the theme of *masking* or *disguise*. Not only does the direc-

tor wear a face "selected without love" (14/28), but the other characters wear an assortment of masks too, beginning with the guards who
wear "doglike" masks (see 13/27, 212/207). Although such masks
would seem to conceal true identity, they ironically serve as a means
of *differentiation* in this world of semblances. As one reads this novel,
one comes across passages in which the narrator seems to slip up
temporarily and to confuse one character with another. The three
principle figures with whom Cincinnatus has to deal in prison are the
director Rodrig Ivanovich, the jailer Rodion, and the lawyer Roman
Vissarionovich. In chapter 3, the figures of the director and the jailer
are momentarily interchanged. When Cincinnatus tries to find out
when he will be executed, the "director" chuckles and says, "Listen
to him. . . . He has to know everything. How do you like that,
Roman Vissarionovich?" After the lawyer sighs his assent, the narrative moves on: " 'Yes, sir,' continued the former, giving his keys a
rattle. 'You ought to be more cooperative, mister' " (39/50). Although the phrase "continued the former" would seem to apply to
the director (Rodrig), the gesture of "giving his keys a rattle" suggests that the speaker is the jailer (Rodion). The latter indication is
then supported by the lawyer's response: he concurs with the
speaker's comments and says, "That's right, Rodion, that right"
(39/51).

This momentary wobble in the narrator's identification of
speakers is soon followed by an even more glaring "mistake." The
jailer Rodion, the lawyer Roman, and Cincinnatus make an excur-
sion to the prison's tower. While there, Rodion sweeps the terrace,
and the narrator notes that the lawyer's back is "soiled with chalk"
(43/54). At the conclusion of the scene, however, we read that it is
the "director" who tosses the broom in a corner and puts his frock
coat on again. The "same little procession" starts back to Cincinnatus's cell: "In front was director Rodrig Ivanovich, behind him
lawyer Roman Vissarionovich, and behind him prisoner Cincinnatus. . . . The back of the director's frock coat was soiled with
chalk" (44/55). Not only have the director and the jailer switched
identities (as in the earlier scene in the cell), but somehow the chalk

from the lawyer's coat has migrated to the back of the director's coat.

Whether the *narrator* is aware of what has happened is not clear, but the reader can no longer regard this as a simple slipup on the *author's* part. Rather, this unexplained shift in identity seems more like that peculiar scene at the beginning of the novel, when the director entered Cincinnatus's cell, only to dissolve and then to reenter. Yet the shift in identity depicted here has a specific function in terms of Nabokov's overall design. It points to an essential feature of the creatures depicted in the novel: these are not unique individuals, but stock, interchangeable characters (or caricatures of characters). In fact, toward the end of the novel, when the artificial world around Cincinnatus is about to become unglued, the director and the lawyer enter Cincinnatus's cell, but they are almost unrecognizable: "without any makeup, without padding and without wigs, with rheumy eyes, with scrawny bodies that one could glimpse through candid rips – they turned out to resemble each other, and their identical heads moved identically on their thin necks" (207/202).

What the reader is dealing with here is a world of complete (and nightmarish) homogeneity, populated by grotesque beings who are identical and interchangeable in their very lifelessness. For Nabokov, this lack of individuality is a prime indication of a flawed and frightening world. In his earlier novel *Despair*, he had had his unbalanced narrator, Hermann Karlovich, envision with fondness such a world, which Hermann imagined was under construction by the Communists in Russia: "Communism shall indeed create a beautifully square world of identical brawny fellows, broad-shouldered and microcephalous."[24]

An additional marker of an underlying uniformity linking the director, the jailer, and the lawyer in *Invitation to a Beheading* is the initial "R" of their names; their names themselves hint at the possibility of a single common ancestor – *Rodion Romanovich Raskolnikov* – the protagonist of Fyodor Dostoevsky's novel *Crime and Punishment*. Nabokov was not a great admirer of Dostoevsky's work; he felt that much of it was marred by implausible character development, crude narrative tricks, and time-worn literary platitudes.[25] He particularly deplored Dostoevsky's depiction of Raskolnikov as a "sensitive murderer" (*SO*, 42). As he viewed it, Raskolnikov's murder of the pawnbroker was "inhuman and idiotic," and Dostoevsky's attempt to evoke sympathy from the reader by pairing Raskolnikov with the prostitute Sonia was "a shoddy literary trick, not a masterpiece of pathos and piety."[26] By giving Cincinnatus's tormentors names that evoke Dostoevsky's "filthy murderer," Nabokov both links the three figures to Raskolnikov's "inhuman and idiotic" crime and provides a parodic glimpse of what happens when such a figure himself becomes the jailer, not the accused.[27]

The ringleader of these masked villains is the executioner M'sieur Pierre, a marvelous creation who is perhaps the supreme embodiment of a particular kind of vulgarity known in Russian as *poshlost'* (or *poshlust*, as Nabokov preferred to spell it). In his critical study of the writer Nikolay Gogol, Nabokov provides a ten-page description of *poshlust* and its attributes. Although the meaning of the word can be approached through such terms as "cheap, sham, common . . . sorry, trashy, scurvy, tawdry," the essential trait Nabokov wished to point out was that "*poshlust* is not only the obviously trashy but also the falsely important, the falsely beautiful, the falsely clever, the falsely attractive."[28] Introduced to Cincinnatus as a fellow prisoner, Pierre characterizes himself as possessing "a rare combination of outward sociability and inward delicacy, the art of causerie and the ability to keep silent, playfulness and seriousness" (85/91). He tries to ingratiate himself into Cincinnatus's good favor by regaling the forlorn hero with pathetic jokes, card tricks that do not work, and chess games at which Pierre proves himself to be a desperate cheat. Manifestations of his essential vulgarity include profound narcissism (his wallet is stuffed with pictures of himself, and he has a dozen similar albums at home [see 82–84/88–90]), a penchant for pontification (for example, he praises "the bliss of relieving onself, which some hold to be on a par with the pleasure of love" [153/153]), and an "imaginative tattoo" that is centered on his left nipple: "two green leaves – so that the nipple itself seemed to be a rosebud" (160/160).

The introduction of Pierre as Cincinnatus's "friend" represents a cruel fraud that masks an even more hideous intent. As Pierre explains it, his benevolent society would like the executioner and the condemned man to develop an "atmosphere of warm camaraderie" for "the success of our common undertaking" (173/171). Not content with beheading its victims, this society wants the victim to feel gratitude for the intimacy shown him by the executioner! Nabokov highlights the perversity of this scheme by having Pierre treat Cincinnatus as if the latter were his lover or spouse. He tells Cincinatatus: "I think I know you . . . more intimately than your wife knew you" (161/161); "To me you are as transparent as . . . a blushing bride is transparent to the gaze of an experienced bridegroom" (162/161). A banquet scheduled for the eve of the execution has the trappings of a wedding feast, with one guest calling for a toast: "Bitter, bitter, sweeten it with a kiss" (185/182). Such an attitude makes a mockery both of the sanctity of human life and of romantic attachment itself.

Behind Pierre, as behind Rodion, Rodrig, and Roman, the reader detects the shadows of earlier characters in Russian literature, and Nabokov envelops his creation in these shadows to underscore further Pierre's essential nature. In Pierre's case, the reader is reminded not so much of characters from Dostoevsky's novels as of characters from the work of Nikolay Gogol, the writer whose tales prompted Nabokov's elaborate description of *poshlust*.[29] In particular, Pierre's behavior has affinities with that of several characters in Gogol's great novel *Dead Souls*. Pierre's arrogance and conceit are reminiscent of the memorable braggart and liar Nozdryov. Indeed, the chess game in which Pierre begins to cheat when he sees that he is losing (144–46/144–46) directly echoes a card game in which Nozdryov demonstrates similar behavior. Yet there is also something of Gogol's protagonist Chichikov in Pierre: his cloying sweetness cannot fully mask a ranker smell of inner decay. When Cincinnatus asks Pierre, "Why do you smell like that?" (146/146), one is reminded of Nabokov's description of the "chink in Chichikov's armor, that rusty chink emitting a faint but dreadful smell," which turns out to be "the organic aperture in the devil's armor."[30] As Nabokov suggests, the *poshlust* evinced by Pierre and Chichikov is not harmless: on the contrary, its sinister emanations have a demonic tinge.[31]

Evaluating the essential vapidity of Pierre and the others who torment Cincinnatus, the émigré critic Vladimir Varshavsky spoke for many readers when he stated, "These are souls who are more dead than Gogol's."[32] Cincinnatus himself articulates a similar perception when he comments that he is surrounded by "some sort of wretched specters, not by people" (36/47). Yet the challenge he faces – to cease believing in the credibility of these figures – is not easily overcome. To assist him in his quest, Nabokov populates his world with a series of objects and creatures who provide models either to emulate or to avoid.

THE SPIDER AND THE MOTH

One such pair of opposing entities is the *spider* and the *moth* Cincinnatus observes in his cell.[33] The spider, an obvious emblem of the predatory world that seeks to keep Cincannatus bound tightly in its grasp, is present in Cincinnnatus's cell from the outset of the novel. Ironically called "official friend of the jailed" (13/27), it is regularly fed and nurtured by Rodion. The spider's sinister work reflects the activities of other figures in the novel, from Pierre (another "official friend"), who is depicted at one point walking around Cincinnatus "as if enmeshing him in something" (160/160),[34] to Cincinnatus's wife Marthe, who began committing adultery soon after their marriage and who continued to entertain lovers while Cincinnatus languished in prison. Cincinnatus himself notes a certain resemblance between Marthe and the spider. How so? It is not simply that the spider moves "with the same resourcefulness as Marthe displayed" in her domestic arrangements (119/121). More important, the spider's fatal web stands as an apt metaphor for Marthe's effect on Cincinnatus. Despite his immense dismay over her incessant infidelities, Cincinnatus loves his wife and longs to return to her, hoping against hope to find something human and vital within her (see 140–42/141–43). At the end of the novel, though, Cincinnatus and the reader learn that this spider is itself artificial, "[c]rudely but cleverly made" (210/205). Its semblance of life represents just one more hoax in a long series of deceptions that have entrapped Cincinnatus in this world.

In contrast to the artificial and predatory spider is a fabulous moth that Rodion intends to feed to the spider but that eludes the jailer instead. This episode, which occurs near the end of the novel, contains a powerful message of encouragement for Cincinnatus, and it proves inspirational in several ways. First, the moth's refusal to play the role of meek victim for the predatory spider foreshadows Cincinnatus's ultimate stand at the end of the novel; in both cases, the intended victim's rejection of his assigned role terrifies his oppressors. Morever, the way the moth "disappeared" – "as if the very air had swallowed it" (204/199) – hints at a fundamental link between the moth and Cincinnatus; at an earlier moment in the novel Cincinnatus is described as so elusive that it seemed he would at any moment "slip naturally and effortlessly through some chink of the air into its unknown coulisses to disappear there" (121/124). Finally, unlike the crudely made toy spider, this moth is ardently alive and is wondrously formed: its wings are termed "visionary" and its overall appearance is "enchanting" (206/201).

The moth's appearance in Cincinnatus's cell and its capacity to avoid destruction comes at a crucial moment in the development of Cincinnatus's ability to resist his captors' designs. The episode occurs as Cincinnatus works on some notes he has been making in his attempt to grapple with his fear and to find a solution to his plight (see the section "Language and Literature" below). The appearance of the moth may in some mysterious way facilitate Cincinnatus's understanding of the correct path he must follow. Nabokov had utilized a moth's sudden appearance for similar purposes in an early short story entitled "Christmas" ("Rozhdestvo," written in 1924). The protagonist of that story, a man named Sleptsov, is so distraught over the untimely death of a beloved son that he himself contemplates suicide. Paralyzed with grief, Sleptsov is startled by a sudden snapping sound. Opening his eyes, he realizes that one of his son's possessions – a cocoon which he believed contained only a dead chrysalid – has been warmed by the room to which he had brought it, and out of it now emerges a huge moth. The moth "miraculously" expands and takes a breath under the impulse of "tender, ravishing, almost human happiness."[35] The emergence of this moth provides a tangible sign that not all is lost with death and that something of the son's spirit remains inviolable and immortal. In Nabokov's subsequent works as well, butterflies and moths often carry such emblematic significance.

The moth, like Cincinnatus, has a genuine, independent life force. From Cincinnatus's perspective, he and the moth may be the only beings who seem truly alive in his world. There is, however, one other character who has at least some inkling of a more authentic reality. This is the woman who presents herself as Cincinnatus's mother in chapter 12. Cincinnatus is initially skeptical: he says that she is "just as much of a parody as everybody and everything else" (132/133). Yet as the woman converses with Cincinnatus, she makes several statements indicating that she has had intuitions of something more substantial and genuine than the sham surroundings that they currently inhabit.[36] For example, she, like Cincinnatus, has intimations of another reality: "[I]t always seems to me," she says, "that a marvelous tale is being repeated over and over again, and I either don't have the time to, or am unable to grasp it, and still somebody keeps repeating it to me, with such patience!" (134/135). This confession is similar to many statements Cincinnatus makes in his written notes (see especially chapter 8).

MIRRORS

What is more, Cincinnatus's mother tells him about a special kind of mirror she saw in her youth, and her description deserves the reader's attention since images of mirrors play a distinctive role in the novel. For the most part, the mirrors that appear in Cincinnatus's world are emblems of the narcissistic tendencies of the figures who populate that world. Many of the characters carry hand mirrors (see, e.g., 21/34 and 99/103), and Pierre waxes eloquently about the pleasures of surrounding oneself with mirrors during lovemaking in order to "watch the good work going on" (145/145). When Marthe makes her first visit to Cincinnatus's cell, she is accompanied by a roomful of furniture, including a "mirrored wardrobe" that contains in "its own private reflection" signs of her continuing infidelity (a dropped glove that is presumably the mate for one carried by Marthe's solicitous escort [cf. 99/104 and 105/110]).

In contrast to these mirrors, which the people of Cincinnatus's world use for narcissistic purposes, are mirrors that appear in passages where the narrator attempts to describe Cincinnatus's elusive personality. For example, in the passage quoted above about Cincinnatus's potential ability to slip effortlessly "through some chink of the air," the narrator notes that Cincinnatus might disappear "with the same easy smoothness with which the flashing reflection of a rotated mirror moves across every object in the room and suddenly vanishes, as if beyond the air" (121/124). This image in turn harks back to a passage in Cincinnatus's notes in which he tries to convey his sense that a higher and better world exists somewhere beyond the confines of the present one: "[T]here everything pleases one's soul, everything is filled with the kind of fun that children know, *there* shines the mirror that now and then sends a chance reflection here" (94/100). In passages such as these, mirror images are used to evoke a sense of momentary but intense illumination, an emblem of something beyond the horizon of immediate vision or knowledge.

The mirror image introduced by Cincinnatus's mother, however, invokes yet a third type of vision and cognition. She speaks of a special kind of mirror to be used with peculiar objects called *nonnons*. Both the objects and the mirror to be used in conjunction with the objects were "completely distorted"; yet "when you placed one of these incomprehensible, monstrous objects so that it was reflected in the incomprehensible, monstrous mirror, a marvelous thing happened; minus by minus equalled plus, everything was restored, everything was fine, and the shapeless speckledness became in the mirror a wonderful, sensible image; flowers, a ship, a person, a landscape" (135–36/137). Many readers find in this image an apt metaphor for the way Nabokov's own art (and particularly this novel) works.[37]

From within the novel, however, Cincinnatus is not sure of the meaning of his mother's description, and he asks her to explain. Instead of responding verbally, his mother merely looks at him, but her intimate gaze carries more meaning than mere words could ever convey in Cincinnatus's sham world: "[I]t was as if something real, unquestionable . . . had passed through, as if a corner of this horrible life had curled up, and there was a glimpse of the lining" (136/137). Cincinnatus suddenly descries "that ultimate, secure, all-explaining and from-all-protecting spark that he knew how to discern in himself also" (136/137). This "spark" proclaimed "such a tumult of truth that Cincinnatus's soul could not help leaping for joy" (136/138). As in the scene with the moth, Cincinnatus gains from this brief interview an electrifying sensation that all is not hopeless and that his aspirations toward a fuller, more authentic life *may* find fulfillment in the days ahead. Yet before Cincinnatus can wholly appreciate the beauty and power of his own inner vision, he must let go of his nostalgic desire to return to the deceptive, disappointing world that continues to ensnare him. One significant marker of Cincinnatus's evolution in this direction is his attitude toward a site of special beauty in his world – the Tamara Gardens.

THE TAMARA GARDENS

Glimpses of the Tamara Gardens crop up repeatedly throughout *Invitation to a Beheading*, and one can observe a distinct shift in the way this locale is perceived and evoked in Cincinnatus's mind. The first extended description of the Gardens occurs in chapter 2, when the major experiences of Cincinnatus's boyhood and youth are recounted for the reader. This description is steeped in warm nostalgia, for it is associated in Cincinnatus's mind with his first romantic interludes – "those rapturous wanderings" – with Marthe (27/40).[38] Yet even here, the discerning reader will note some disquieting elements. For example, on an "idyllic" park bench, "three jokers had left three neat little heaps (it's a trick – they are imitations made of brown painted tin)" (28/40). The alluring vista is spoiled by a trio of trite tricksters.

Cincinnatus gains another glimpse of the Tamara Gardens from the terrace on top of the prison tower. Here, however, he is separated from the Gardens by a considerable distance, and he can only gaze with "vague and perhaps even blissful despair" (43/54). He imagines that he might possibly find a refuge in the hills beyond the Gardens, but he instantly realizes that he had better "not think about it" (43/54). Indeed, for Cincinnatus to imagine a refuge *within* the confines of his present world is to become a coconspirator in his own imprisonment. Not for nothing does the narrator observe that the very structure of Cincinnatus's rib cage "expressed the barred nature of his surroundings, of his gaol" (65/73), or that when Cincinnatus looks toward the grating on the cell window, "there was a tiny golden cage in each of his mirrorlike pupils" (29/41). Cincinnatus's very attachment to people and places in the world around him acts to restrict his capacity to overcome and to transcend that world.

A third evocation of the Tamara Gardens lays bare the potential trap the Gardens represent for Cincinnatus. This evocation is not a description of the Gardens themselves but rather of a painted *representation* of the Gardens that is embedded in a recess in the prison walls. What makes this description significant is that its depiction of the shabby nature of the reproduction points to the fundamental property of the surrounding world at large: "[A]ll of this was somehow not fresh, antiquated, covered with dust" (77/84). As he looks at the scene, Cincinnatus can use his imagination to "recognize" the features depicted in it, but the scene itself is a fraud.

What we find here, then, is a divergence between Cincinnatus's inner vision of the Tamara Gardens and their shoddy incarnation or reproduction in his immediate surroundings. This divergence is characteristic of the broader split that Cincinnatus experiences between his internal intuitions and his perception of the material world that surrounds him. This split reaches a culmination at the ceremonial banquet set for the eve of his execution. Cincinnatus is taken outside to gaze at a landscape that he recognizes as the Tamara

Gardens. There, he "removed the murky film of night from the familiar lawns and also erased from them the superfluous lunar dusting, so as to make them exactly as they were in his memory" (187/184). In contrast to this *inner* recovery, however, Cincinnatus must also witness an *external* illumination of the Gardens: his oppressors have arranged "a good million light bulbs" to be lit up at once, "all arranged in such a way as to embrace the whole nocturnal landscape with a grandiose monogram of 'P' and 'C,' which, however, had not quite come off" (189/187). It is Cincinnatus's exposure to this grotesque desecration of his cherished Gardens – "those hills which broke out in a deadly rash" – that helps him to recognize how the entire external world has "duped" him and to understand that he "should not have sought salvation within its confines" (205/200).

The vision of the Tamara Gardens that Cincinnatus carries within him has no authentic counterpart in the sham world that has imprisoned him. He must harbor no hope of finding peace or fulfillment within its borders. Yet how, then, is he to overcome the lure of these deceptive specters? What resources can he marshall to help him find another path? The answer lies in one of the most important image systems embedded in the text – that of language and literature itself.

LANGUAGE AND LITERATURE

Perhaps the single most comprehensive thematic pattern in *Invitation to a Beheading* centers on *language*, and on the organization of language into *artistic texts*. As D. Barton Johnson demonstrates (see his article in the present volume), Nabokov manipulates the very building blocks of his novel – individual sounds and letters – to give depth and resonance to his creative plan for the work. What is more, the novel explores contrasting modes of expression: on the one hand are the modes utilized by Cincinnatus's society – lifeless and conventional; on the other is Cincinnatus's own aspiration to develop a fresh, meaningful, and evocative language with which he can express his unprecedented intuitions.

One of the leading features of the society that has imprisoned

Cincinnatus is its transparency. This transparency is evident both in terms of physical characteristics (Cincinnatus is the only person who is "opaque") and in terms of its communicative practices: "Those around [Cincinnatus] understood each other at the first word, since they had no words that would end in an unexpected way" (26/38). In this world there are no mysteries left. As the narrator puts it: "*That which does not have a name does not exist*. Unfortunately everything had a name" (26/38; emphasis in the original). As befits a theatrical world, the speeches these people deliver are carefully scripted, and they are heavily formulaic, even to the point of inanity. A striking example of the ultimate lack of content found in the speaking and writing practices of this world is an observation the narrator makes when describing Cincinnatus's lawyer transcribing one of Pierre's speeches. Although Pierre himself has been reading from a script, the lawyer writes down Pierre's remarks. This act of writing has become so automatic that when Pierre stops talking, the lawyer continues mindlessly on: "Silence ensued. The lawyer was writing so quickly that the flashing of his pencil hurt the eyes" (177/175).

What kind of *literature* can such a society produce? During his confinement Cincinnatus has been making his way through a "contemporary novel" entitled *Quercus*, named after its central figure, an oak tree (122/124). The plan of the novel, which is considered "the acme of modern thought" (122/125), is to record everything the oak tree might have witnessed during its centuries of life. As the narrator comments, "It seemed as though the author were sitting with his camera somewhere among the topmost branches of the Quercus, spying out and catching his prey" (123/125). The last phrase of this sentence brings to mind the spider in Cincinnatus's cell. The book itself consists of various narratives overheard from characters passing by, as well as observations on "dendrology, ornithology, coleopterology, mythology" (123/125). What one finds here, as one critic has observed, is "specious metonymy, where all-inclusiveness is made to stand for coherence."[39] That such a farrago of disjointed material would pass for something aesthetically satisfying or valuable in Cincinnatus's society is a telling comment about the aesthetic tastes (or lack of taste) of that society.[40] Robert Alter declares this novel to be "Nabokov's *reductio ad absurdum* of the naturalistic novel," and he argues that such photographic realism "is mindless, formless, pointless, infinitely tedious, devoid of humanity."[41] It is fitting, then, that Cincinnatus finds the entire production "distant, deceitful and dead" (123/126).[43]

Cincinnatus's quest is to find another means of verbal expression, one that will ultimately lead him out of the "dead end" of this world (205/200). Nabokov's novel (a work entirely unlike *Quercus*) follows Cincinnatus in this task. The quest begins at the very outset of the novel, when Cincinnatus is brought to his cell and finds there a clean sheet of paper. He immediately begins writing: "In spite of everything I am comparatively. After all I had premonitions, had premonitions of this finale" (12–13/26). At this early juncture, Cincinnatus is unable to set down his thoughts in a clear, orderly way. His fear and anxiety entirely rule his being. Indeed, he senses Rodion's spying gaze behind him, and thus he "crossed out what he had written" (13/26). As time passes, however, he begins to master his anxiety and to channel his thoughts into more lucid and poetic forms. This is already evident in his second attempt to record his thoughts. Although he begins with disjointed fragments ("But then perhaps [. . .] I am misinterpreting . . . Attributing to the epoch . . . This wealth . . . Torrents" [51/61]), he soon settles into longer and more cogent phrases, such as when he tries to convey his sense of his own uniqueness: "I am not an ordinary – I am the one among you who is alive – Not only are my eyes different, and my hearing, and my sense of taste – not only is my sense of smell like a deer's . . . but, most important, I have the capacity to conjoin all of this in one point" (52/62).

The most extended exposition both of Cincinnatus's quest to find the proper words for his inner vision, and of that inner vision itself, occurs in chapter 8, which consists almost entirely of Cincinnatus's writing. One of the most striking things to emerge from this passage is Cincinnatus's fervent belief in the existence of another, better realm, of which his present world is only a crude imitation. He writes: "It exists, my dream world, it must exist, since, surely there must be an original of the clumsy copy" (93/99); "*There, tam, là-bas*, the gaze of men glows with inimitable understanding. . . . *There*, *there* are the originals of those gardens where we used to roam . . . *there* everything strikes one by its bewitching evidence, by the simplicity of perfect good . . . *there* shines the mirror that now and then sends a chance reflection here" (94/99–100).[43]

As noted above, Cincinnatus's intuition of the existence of another, more perfect realm has reminded many readers of the teachings of Gnostic and Neoplatonic philosophy. Cincinnatus's notes in chapter 8 contain numerous images that have counterparts in early Gnostic texts (e.g., "I am like a pearl ring embedded in a shark's gory fat" [90/95]).[44] At the same time, however, one should avoid the temptation to interpret the novel too narrowly in a Gnostic context. Nabokov's own worldview entails a greater appreciation for the beauty of the *physical* world than a strict Gnostic approach would support, and the metaphysical vision that underpins his work has a broad, syncretic sweep.[45] Nonetheless, he makes use of the dualism found in Gnosticism to underscore the disparity between Cincinnatus's tawdry, flawed, imitative world and the more alluring world sensed in his dreams.

Although Cincinnatus possesses a rich intuition of another realm, he feels frustrated by his inability to put this intuition into words. As he states early in chapter 8, "I know something. I know something. But expression of it comes so hard!" (91/96). Later, he laments: "Alas, no one taught me this kind of chase, and the ancient inborn art of writing is long since forgotten – forgotten are the days when it needed no schooling, but ignited and blazed like a forest fire" (93/98).[46] Cincinnatus longs for a receptive audience but recognizes that since "there is in the world not a single human who can speak my language; or, more simply, not a single human who can speak; or, even more simply, not a single human; I must think only of myself" (95/100).

His task for the remainder of the novel is to work on the realization of his intuitions. On the one hand, he must cease looking to the shallow beings around him for salvation. As the narrator puts it, Cincinnatus himself "inspired the meaningless with meaning, and the lifeless with life" (155/155). Again and again, Cincinnatus finds himself imagining the assistance of someone nearby, and often these episodes reveal a fallacious reliance on literary models from the past. Thus, for example, he hopes the director's daughter Emmie will help him escape from prison: "I wondered, *to the rhythm of an ancient poem* – could she not give the guards a drugged potion, could she not rescue me? If only she would remain the child she is, but at the same time mature and understand – and then it would be feasible: her burning cheeks, a black windy night, salvation, salvation" (53/63; emphasis added).[47] Not only is Cincinnatus mistaken in wishing that this child would suddenly "mature and understand" (this would entail, in its own way, the kind of false maturation implied in Pierre's vulgar "photohoroscope" of Emmie; see 170–71/168–69), but he repeats an error made by other Nabokovian protagonists: any attempt to live one's life based on old literary models is doomed to end in failure.[48] Nor can the literature of the past itself provide a needed refuge in and of itself. Early in the novel the narrator describes Cincinnatus making dolls for schoolgirls – "little hairy Pushkin," "ratlike Gogol," and so on – and he comments, "Having *artificially* developed a fondness for this *mythical* Nineteenth Century, Cincinnatus was ready to become completely engrossed in the mists of that antiquity and find therein a *false* shelter, but something else distracted him" (27/39–40; emphasis added). The "something else" was Marthe.

What Cincinatus must do is to suspend his willingness to believe in the value and viability of the beings around him and to develop the nascent spark of originality and creativity that he senses within himself. In this endeavor, an appreciation of literary art *does* provide some assistance. Toward the end of the narrative Cincinnatus writes: "Envious of poets. How wonderful it must be to speed along a page and, right from the page, where only a shadow continues to run, to take off into the blue" (194/190). In an uncanny way, Cincinnatus here scripts the denouement of his own story as a condemned man.

The image of the running shadow looks forward to the scene of Cincinnatus's "execution," which results in his departure for another realm. It is also in this set of notes that Cincinnatus indicates his growing awareness of the proper direction in which to channel his energies. He writes: "I must have at least the theoretical possibility of having a reader, otherwise, really, I might as well tear it all up. There, that is what I needed to say. Now it is time to get ready" (194/190). Instead of looking for support from the weird "dummies" who surround him, Cincinnatus realizes the need to reach out toward a different, more substantial audience – those who can appreciate fresh, original texts, works of authentic art.

Cincinnatus's final written record confirms the maturation both of his inner knowledge and of his understanding of the best means for articulating that knowledge. He begins this note just after the fabulous moth has escaped Rodion's grasp. He acknowledges that he has been duped by the surrounding world and that he should not have sought salvation "within its confines" (205/200). Recognizing the danger of misarticulation, he notes that "it is best to leave some things unsaid, or else I shall get confused again" (205/200). Finally, he writes that he is now almost fearless of "death," but, as soon as he finishes that word, he crosses it out, feeling that he should find a more precise term for his thought. He walks away from the table, leaving on it "the blank sheet with only the one solitary word on it, and that one crossed out" (206/200). Significantly, he never returns to the note, for Pierre and his henchmen come to take him to his execution. At first, Cincinnatus pleads for more time to "finish writing something," but then he pauses and suddenly realizes "that everything had in fact been written already" (209/204).

Cincinnatus's insight here is highly significant, as is the remarkable notation he has left on the sheet of paper. This sign – the word *death* crossed out – represents the culmination of a series of motifs that run through the novel. First, Cincinnatus's gesture of crossing out the word *death* echoes his handling of his first written note in chapter 1 (see 13/26). In that instance, however, he was driven by *fear* to cross out what he had written. Here, in contrast, he does so out of a calm determination to find the best means of expressing his inner vision. Moreover, in the act of canceling something that already represents a kind of negation ("death" as the end of life), Cincinnatus reproduces the effect of the *nonnon* objects and mirror: "minus by minus equaled plus, everything was restored, everything was fine" (135/137). For him, there will be no "death" as it is generally understood. On the contrary, he will ascend to another, more fulfilling mode of existence. It is also meaningful that he has not entirely erased the word *death*. Rather, his written sign contains *both* the word *and* its cancellation. This creates a marvelous emblem for the climactic scene of the novel itself – a beheading that is also, in its own way, a nonbeheading.

The scene of Cincinnatus's execution has occasioned much commentary. Some critics have argued that Cincinnatus *is* beheaded; others claim that he is *not*. The evidence planted in the text supports both claims. On the one hand, the observation that the librarian is vomiting on the steps would suggest that he is reacting to the sight of a bloody decapitation. On the other hand, Cincinnatus is depicted "getting up and looking around" (222/217). Perhaps the best way to understand the scene is to imagine that Cincinnatus both *is* and *is not* beheaded. Or, to put it another way, *one* form of Cincinnatus is beheaded, while *another* form survives or is set free. As the narrator formulates it, "[O]ne Cincinnatus was counting, but the other Cincinnatus had already stopped heeding the sound of the unnecessary count . . . and with a clarity he had never experienced before . . . he reflected: why am I here? Why am I lying like this?" (222/217). *This* Cincinnatus gets up, looks around, and finally makes his way "in that direction where, to judge by the voices, stood beings akin to him" (223/218), while the painted world around him collapses in a heap.

Throughout the novel, Nabokov's narrator mentions the presence of a "double" within Cincinnatus, defining this as "the double, the gangrel, that accompanies each of us – you, and me, and him over there – doing what we would like to do at that very moment, but cannot" (25/37). Presumably, one of the two Cincinnatuses – that aspect of his personality which tends to cling to the world and gives credence to the shallow dummies around him – is beheaded, while the other – that aspect which nurtures its inner vision and senses the existence of a better realm – survives and moves out of this unstable, artificial world.[49]

To what kind of realm does the liberated Cincinnatus go? Nabokov leaves the answer deliberately unclear. The one detail he *does* provide is that the beings akin to Cincinnatus have "voices." Throughout the novel Cincinnatus has been struggling to find his own autonomous voice. Those who wish to see Cincinnatus's growth primarily as the maturation of a writer may conclude that Cincinnatus is now ready to join those who have "voices" – that is, tellers of tales. On the other hand, those who focus on the spiritual implications of Cincinnatus's growth may take note of the fact that one other figure in the novel is referred to only by his "voice" – Cincinnatus's father. As Cincinnatus's mother tells it, she never saw the man who became Cincinnatus's father; she only heard his voice (133/134). Sergej Davydov points out that this aura of unknowability links Cincinnatus's father with "the Gnostic notion of an unknowable God, called 'the Alien,' 'the nameless,' 'the Hidden,' or 'the Unknown Father.'"[50] Other critics have detected in the mother's report a parodic allusion to the Christian notion of the Immaculate Conception.[51] Indeed, Cincinnatus himself sardonically wonders what trade his unseen father could have had: might he have been "a carpenter" (133/134)? From this perspective, the scene in which Cincinnatus rises up from the chopping block sends out distant echoes of the death and resurrection of Jesus Christ, but one must be careful not to exaggerate the significance of these echoes.[52]

The conclusion Nabokov provides for his novel is remarkably open-ended. The evidence suggests that Cincinnatus passes into the kind of transcendent realm that had been beckoning to him in his dreams throughout the novel, but it is up to the individual reader to speculate on the precise nature of that realm. By ending the novel in this way, Nabokov confers on his hero a type of immortality or timelessness in the mind of the reader. Here, the metaphysical and metaliterary dimensions of Nabokov's work come together, and each of these dimensions gains depth from the other. No matter what specific associations the conclusion of *Invitation to a Beheading* suggests to a reader, the scene itself provides a bracing celebration of human courage and of the indomitable will to strive for freedom in the face of long odds. As such, it represents a milestone in Nabokov's career. To place this work in perspective, we should now consider the context in which it was written.

Invitation to a Beheading and Nabokov's Career

The genesis of *Invitation to a Beheading* reflects the confluence of several creative strands in Nabokov's career. As a native of St. Petersburg (where he was born in 1899), Nabokov could lay claim to a rich literary and cultural heritage. St. Petersburg had figured prominently in the work of Pushkin, Gogol, and Dostoevsky, and it would remain an emblem for cultural refinement even after the Russian Revolution.[53] The first decade of the twentieth century saw a lush flowering of the arts, both in Petersburg and Moscow. Nabokov himself was raised in a highly cultured and cosmopolitan household. His father, a distinguished jurist with democratic leanings, entertained many foreign visitors, including H. G. Wells.[54] In his youth Nabokov was exposed to a wide range of literature, from Jules Verne and Conan Doyle, to Flaubert, Gogol, Chekhov, and Tolstoy.[55] He particularly savored the work of the Symbolist and post-Symbolist poets, from Alexander Blok to Nikolay Gumilyov.

Although he would later deny the influence of any writer on his work (*SO*, 116), Nabokov shared with his contemporaries a special interest in the way that individual human consciousness perceives and interprets the phenomena of human existence. Indeed, he vehemently rejected the idea that so-called average reality, the reality "perceived by all of us," is "true reality." He declared: "Average reality begins to rot and stink as soon as the act of individual creation ceases to animate a subjectively perceived texture" (*SO*, 118). It is no surprise, then, that he would tell an interviewer that his "masterpieces of twentieth century prose" were Joyce's *Ulysses*, Kafka's *Meta-*

morphosis, Andrey Bely's *Petersburg*, and Proust's *A la recherche du temps perdu* (see *SO*, 57).[56] By the time he wrote *Invitation to a Beheading*, Nabokov had already created a memorable series of works that explored the unique dimensions of subjective reality. These works include the short story "Terra Incognita" (1931), which contrasts a man's vibrant dreams about an exotic jungle milieu with the more mundane setting of a European bedroom, where he apparently lies dying with a fever,[57] and the novels *The Eye* and *Despair. Despair* (written in 1932; published in 1934) features a man who believes he has found his identical double; after killing the supposed double and trying to assume his identity, he reveals that the police investigating the crime find absolutely no similarity between the murderer and victim. *The Eye* (published in 1930) focuses on the impressions of a man who attempts to commit suicide, claims that the attempt is successful, and spends his post-death existence by spying on a number of other characters, including a figure named Smurov, who, the reader surmises, is none other than the narrator himself. Apparently the suicide attempt has failed, and the man is attempting to delude himself and the reader into believing that his consciousness lives on after death.

In all these works one finds a recurrent theme that also informs *Invitation to a Beheading* – the desire (to paraphrase a comment made by a character in Nabokov's *Pale Fire*) to "peel off a drab and unhappy past and replace it with a brilliant invention."[58] Many of Nabokov's characters are solitary, unappreciated individuals who seek to leave behind their mundane existences and to enter a more beautiful and wondrous space instead. Reminiscent of Cincinnatus is the title character of the story "Lik" (written in 1938). A lonely Russian émigré working as an actor in France, Lik feels he has been "condemned to live on the outskirts of life."[59] He has a persistent fantasy of passing into the world of the play in which he currently performs: he would then "find himself in a world of ineffable tenderness – a bluish, delicate world where fabulous adventures of the senses occur, and unheard-of metamorphoses of the mind."[60] As part of this fantasy, Lik imagines dying on stage, but his "death," like that of Cincinnatus, would take him beyond the confines of the stage setting in which he performs: "[H]e would not notice his death, crossing over instead into the actual world of a chance play, now blooming anew because of his arrival, while his smiling corpse lay on the boards, the toe of one foot protruding from beneath the folds of the lowered curtain."[61]

The reader never learns whether Lik manages to enter the radiant "otherworld" for which he longs, but the hope that death will not mean the cessation of being itself is a central concern of Nabokov's art. Many of his works reveal his interest in the possibility that something of the human spirit may survive and even expand after death. The author resisted the idea that human consciousness – rich, vital, throbbing with life – is snuffed out at death. Writing of his love for his wife and son in *Speak, Memory*, he reveals his dismay over the very notion of mortality: "I have to have all space and all time participate in my emotion, in my mortal love, so that the edge of its mortality is taken off, thus helping me to fight the utter degradation, ridicule, and horror of *having developed an infinity of sensation and thought within a finite existence*."[62] His enduring antipathy toward the idea that death brings nothing but oblivion filters through much of his later work, particularly *Pale Fire* (published in 1962) and *Transparent Things* (published in 1972), which is narrated by a ghost.

Nabokov's impulse to fight against the "black void" (*Speak, Memory*, 20) undoubtedly took on added urgency after his father was killed while trying to stop a political assassination in 1922.[63] The specter of his father's death, and the hope that his father's spirit would remain a vital presence in his life, informs much of Nabokov's writing. In the poem "Evening on a Vacant Lot" (1932) Nabokov writes of seeing his father approach across an empty lot at twilight: "I recognize / your energetic stride. You haven't / changed much since you died."[64] The protagonist of Nabokov's novel *The Gift*, Fyodor Godunov-Cherdyntsev, also has a vision of his missing father's return at a pivotal moment in the tale.

It was during his work on *The Gift* that Nabokov began writing *Invitation to a Beheading*, and the reader finds in *The Gift* several specific elements that may have shaped the writer's approach to this novel. *The Gift* depicts a young writer, Fyodor Godunov-Cherdyntsev, developing and refining his creative talents. One of the writer's projects is a biography of the nineteenth-century critic Nikolay Chernyshevsky, a figure often associated with the notion that literature should serve the interests of society and that a work of art is essentially inferior to material reality. Chernyshevsky was imprisoned for his radical activism, and he underwent a mock execution before being sent into exile in Siberia.

The relevance of Nabokov's research on this topic for the genesis of *Invitation to a Beheading* is clear. In *The Gift* Nabokov has Fyodor recall his father declaring that "innate in every man is the feeling of something insuperably abnormal about the death penalty, something like the uncanny reversal of action in a looking glass."[65] This image of abnormality and distortion returns at the end of the passage: "[I]n China it was precisely *an actor* – a shadow – who fulfilled the duties of the executioner, all responsibility being as it were lifted from the world of men *and transformed into the inside-out one of mirrors*" (*The Gift*, 215; emphasis added). Nabokov has taken these images and given them life in *Invitation to a Beheading*.[66]

A second element found in *The Gift* also influenced the contours of Nabokov's creation in *Invitation*. Studying a Soviet chess magazine, Fyodor notices some flaws in the chess problems printed there, and he suddenly reflects: "[W]hy had everything in Russia become so shoddy, so crabbed and gray, how could she have been so befooled and befuddled?" (*The Gift*, 187). This resonates with Cincinnatus's perception that his "terrible, striped world" seems "not a bad example of amateur craftsmanship, but is in reality calamity, horror, madness, error" (91/96). What is more, in response to his dismay over what has befallen Russia, Fyodor wonders: "Ought one not to reject any longing for one's homeland, for any homeland besides that which is with me, within me . . . ?" (*The Gift*, 187). This is precisely Cincinnatus's mission – to reject his longing for a return to the "homeland" that has deceived him and to nurture instead his inner vision of a more perfect and fulilling realm.[67]

Near the end of *The Gift*, Fyodor envisions translating a novel by "an old French sage" (*The Gift*, 376). As D. Barton Johnson and others have argued, this French sage is surely "Pierre Delaland," a philosopher Nabokov invented.[68] Several of Delaland's reflections on death are included in *The Gift*, and a quotation from his work, *Discours sur les ombres*, serves as the epigraph to *Invitation to a Beheading*: "Comme un fou se croit Dieu, nous nous croyons mortels" ("As a madman believes himself God, we believe ourselves mortal," 10). *Invitation to a Beheading*, then, may be that novel by an old French sage that "Fyodor" has translated "in [his] own manner" (see *The Gift*, 376).[69]

The image of a "terrible, striped world" in *Invitation to a Beheading* not only reflects Nabokov's dismay over the noxious effects of the Soviet regime in his former homeland but also his apprehension about the rising tide of prejudice and repression in his current place of residence, Germany.[70] In several works of the mid- to late 1930s, including *Invitation*, Nabokov targets an attribute of such regimes that he found particularly repugnant: the attempt of the collective to make an individual join in its activities and to do so with a kind of artificially pumped-up enthusiasm that thinly veils an underlying menace. In the short story "The Leonardo" ("Korolek," published in 1933), two beefy brothers harass and finally kill an enigmatic, solitary figure who tries to elude their prying gaze[71]; in "Cloud, Castle, Lake" ("Ozero, oblako, bashnia," published in 1937), a mild Russian émigré is forced to participate in the simpleminded activities of a group of Germans on a "pleasure trip." When the man tries to drop out of the group, he is forced to remain with the collective and is savagely beaten by the group on the return journey: "All had a wonderful time." Before he is dragged away, the poor victim protests to his tormentors: "[T]his is nothing less than an invitation to a beheading."[72]

Nabokov's readers have often compared his portrayal of an oppressive collective *Invitation to a Beheading* to the corresponding novel he finished in 1946, *Bend Sinister* (published in 1947). Nabokov himself characterized these novels as "the two bookends of grotesque design between which my other volumes tightly huddle" (*SO*, 287). Completed after the full extent of the Nazi horror had been exposed to the world, *Bend Sinister* portrays an oppressive and sadistic regime in a tone that is, in places, considerably more somber than the tone of *Invitation to a Beheading*. The sense of triumph with which the earlier novel concludes is not matched in the later work. Whereas Cincinnatus achieves a clear victory over his captors and exits a world collapsing behind him, the protagonist of *Bend Sinister*, Adam Krug, is saved from death only by the sudden intervention of the narrator who abruptly breaks off his narrative to investigate a moth striking the window screen of his room. The narrator confesses: "I knew that the immortality I had conferred on the poor fellow was a slippery sophism, a play upon words. But the very last lap of his life had been happy and it had been proven to him that death was but a question of style."[73]

This shift in tone may not only reflect a more sober understanding of the full savagery that a nation's tyranny can attain; it may also reflect a change in Nabokov's own life. His son Dmitri had been born in 1934 (not long before *Invitation to a Beheading* was composed), and Nabokov's love for his growing child may have made him aware that the potential for destroying a person's happiness was even greater than he had imagined earlier. Thus Krug in *Bend Sinister* is informed that his son has been beaten and killed in a horrific, experimental therapy for the criminally insane, and he is made to watch the beginning of a film in which this depraved torture is depicted. Evaluating *Invitation to a Beheading*, some readers have questioned the plausibility of the premise they detect in the novel – that an individual's imagination has the power to escape and even bring down a totalitarian regime.[74] Although reading the novel in this way tends to overemphasize its ideological implications at the expense of other aspects, Leona Toker has noted in her study of Nabokov that the writer would explore a similar premise in his 1938 story, "Tyrants Destroyed" ("Istreblenie tiranov"). *Bend Sinister*, Toker declares, demonstrates conclusively the "insufficiency" of such a premise.[75]

By 1934, however, Nazi Germany had not yet revealed the full measure of its viciousness, and Nabokov himself was filled with the twin joys of creative inspiration and new parenthood. It was in this spirit that he fashioned his "violin in a void," and one can be sure that, true to Nabokov's dream, more than a few readers of *Invitation to a Beheading* will, upon finishing the novel, "jump up, ruffling their hair" (8).

NOTES

1. Vladimir Nabokov, *Strong Opinions* (New York: McGraw-Hill, 1973), 76, 92. All further citations from this book will be noted by a parenthetical reference in the text with the abbreviation *SO* and the relevant page number.

2. The preceding novels were *Mary* (*Mashen'ka*), *King, Queen, Knave* (*Korol', Dama, Valet*), *The Defense* (*Zashchita Luzhina*), *The Eye* (*Sogliadatai*), *Glory* (*Podvig*), *Camera Obscura* (*Kamera obskura*, which Nabokov later translated and reworked with the title *Laughter in the Dark*), and *Despair* (*Otchaianie*).

3. Vladimir Nabokov, *Invitation to a Beheading* (New York: Vintage International, 1989), 72; cf. *Priglashenie na kazn'* (Ann Arbor, Mich.: Ardis, 1979), 80. All subsequent page references to these editions will be given in the text in the following form: (English page number / Russian page number). The English translation was prepared by Nabokov's son Dmitri in collaboration with the author. As Robert Hughes has noted, this novel "seems to have suffered least change in the process of conversion"; see "Notes on the Translation of *Invitation to a Beheading*," *TriQuarterly* 17 (1970): 285. Jane Grayson expresses a similar opinion in *Nabokov Translated: A Comparison of Nabokov's Russian and English Prose* (Oxford: Oxford University Press, 1977), 120. For a discussion of some of the discrepancies between the Russian and English texts, see D. Barton Johnson's article "The Alpha and Omega of Nabokov's *Invitation to a Beheading*" in the present volume.

4. The novel was published in *Sovremennye zapiski* from June 1935 to February 1936. It came out in book form in 1938 and was published in English translation in 1959.

5. Among the most insightful contemporary responses were the articles by Vladislav Khodasevich, "On Sirin," trans. Michael H Walker, ed. Simon Karlinsky and Robert P. Hughes, *TriQuarterly* 17 (1970): 96–101; and by

P. M. Bitsilli, "V. Nabokov's *Invitation to a Beheading* and *The Eye*," trans.
D. Barton Johnson, in *A Book of Things about Vladimir Nabokov*, ed. Carl R.
Proffer (Ann Arbor, Mich.: Ardis, 1974), 65–69. For a brief survey of contemporary émigré reactions to the novel, see Ludmila A. Foster, "Nabokov's
Gnostic Turpitude: The Surrealistic Vision of Reality in *Priglašenie na
kazn'*," in *Mnemozina: Studia litteraria russica in honorem Vsevolod Setchkarev*,
ed. Joachim T. Baer and Norman W. Ingham (Munich: Fink, 1974), 117–18.

6. Natalya Reznikova, quoted by Andrew Field in *Nabokov: His Life in Art*
(Boston: Little, Brown, 1967), 190. Nabokov's pseudonym "Sirin" refers to a
mythological bird found in Russian folklore; it is also one name for the
Snowy Owl (see *SO*, 161).

7. V. S. Varshavskii, *Nezamechennoe pokolenie* (New York: Chekhov, 1956),
218.

8. See Rampton, *Vladimir Nabokov: A Critical Study of the Novels* (Cambridge: Cambridge University Press, 1984), 31–63.

9. Gary Saul Morson, *The Boundaries of Genre: Dostoevsky's Diary of a
Writer and the Traditions of Literary Utopia* (Austin: University of Texas Press,
1981), 116.

10. See, e.g., Renata Galtseva and Irina Rodnyanskaya, "The Obstacle:
The Human Being, or the Twentieth Century in the Mirror of Dystopia,"
South Atlantic Quarterly vol. 90, no. 2 (1991): 293–322; Sergej Davydov,
"*Invitation to a Beheading*" in *The Garland Companion to Vladimir Nabokov*, ed.
Vladimir E. Alexandrov (New York: Garland, 1995), 201 n. 7; Laurie Clancy,
The Novels of Vladimir Nabokov (New York: St. Martin's, 1984), 65; and
Rampton, *Vladimir Nabokov*, 52–53.

11. In the foreword to *Despair* he asserts: "*Despair*, in kinship with the
rest of my books, has no social comment to make, no message to bring in its
teeth. It does not uplift the spiritual organ of man, nor does it show humanity the right exit" (Vladimir Nabokov, *Despair* [New York: G. P. Putnam's
Sons, 1966], 8).

12. Nabokov himself, however, was not oblivious to the political implications of his accomplishment in *Invitation to a Beheading*. He termed this
novel and his later novel *Bend Sinister* "absolutely final indictments of Russian and German totalitarianism" (*SO*, 156). Cognizant of the unique nature
of Nabokov's design in *Invitation to a Beheading*, Leona Toker has suggested
that with this novel Nabokov produced a parody *both* on the utopian struc-

tures of totalitarian states *and* on the inventions of writers of *dystopian novels*; see *Nabokov: The Mystery of Literary Structures* (Ithaca, N.Y.: Cornell University Press, 1989), 140.

13. On the other hand, Nabokov was not the cold aesthete that some critics have perceived him to be. Nabokov himself offered a humorous re-evaluation of his reputation along these lines: "I believe that one day a reappraiser will come and declare that far from having been a frivolous firebird, I was a rigid moralist kicking sin, cuffing stupidity, ridiculing the vulgar and cruel – and assigning sovereign power to tenderness, talent, and pride" (*SO*, 193). For an interesting treatment of the disparate forces at work in Nabokov's art, see Michael Wood, *The Magician's Doubts: Nabokov and the Risks of Fiction* (Princeton, N.J.: Princeton University Press, 1995).

14. Khodasevich, "On Sirin," 100.

15. See Pifer, *Nabokov and the Novel* (Cambridge, Mass.: Harvard University Press, 1980), 49–67; and Toker, *Nabokov*, 123–41.

16. See Julian Moynahan, "A Russian Preface for Nabokov's *Beheading*," *Novel* 1 (1967): 12–18; Robert Grossmith, "Spiralizing the Circle: The Gnostic Subtext in Nabokov's *Invitation to a Beheading*," *Essays in Poetics* 12.2 (1987): 51–74; Sergej Davydov, *"Teksty-Matreški" Vladimira Nabokova* (Munich: Otto Sagner, 1982), 100–182; and Sergej Davydov, "*Invitation to a Beheading*," in *The Garland Companion to Vladimir Nabokov*, 188–203.

17. Toker, *Nabokov*, 129.

18. Vladimir Nabokov, "Good Readers and Good Writers," *Lectures on Literature*, 3.

19. Nabokov, "Good Readers and Good Writers," 1.

20. The most detailed discussion of the theatrical motifs in the novel is found in Dabney Stuart, *Nabokov: The Dimensions of Parody* (Baton Rouge: Louisiana State University Press, 1978), 58–67.

21. See Nabokov, *Speak, Memory* (New York: G. P. Putnam's Sons, 1966), 278–79.

22. Vladimir Nabokov, *The Annotated Lolita*, ed. Alfred Appel, Jr. (New York: Vintage, 1991), 302.

23. The show trials targeted against engineers and professors in 1928, 1930, 1931, and 1933 were followed by the even more sensational trials of Old Bolsheviks from 1936 to 1938. For a detailed account of those trials, see Robert Conquest, *The Great Terror: Stalin's Purge of the Thirties* (New York:

Macmillan, 1968). Joel Carmichael highlights the theatrical aspects of the show trials in his *Stalin's Masterpiece: The Show Trials and Purges of the Thirties – the Consolidation of the Bolshevik Dictatorship* (New York: St. Martin's, 1976).

24. Nabokov, *Despair*, 30; see also *Despair*, 169: "I visualize . . . a world where the worker fallen dead at the feet of his machine will be at once replaced by his perfect double smiling the serene smile of perfect socialism."

25. One of Nabokov's most memorable pronouncements on Dostoevsky reads: "He was a prophet, a claptrap journalist and a slapdash comedian" (*SO*, 42). A more detailed critique of Dostoevsky's strengths and weaknesses can be found in Nabokov's *Lectures on Russian Literature*, ed. Fredson Bowers (New York: Harcourt Brace Jovanovich / Bruccoli Clark, 1981), 97–135.

26. Nabokov, *Lectures on Russian Literature*, 110.

27. The patronymics that some of the characters have also carry suspicious associations. The name "Roman Vissarionovich" conjures up Stalin's name – "Iosif Vissarionovich" – and a figure who appears only by name – "Arkady Ilyich" (25/38) – has the same patronymic as Lenin, whose name was "Vladimir Ilyich."

28. Vladimir Nabokov, *Nikolai Gogol* (New York: New Directions, 1961), 64, 70.

29. Critics have, however, detected Dostoevskian echoes in Pierre's character, too. Pekka Tammi notes a "certain resemblance" to Porfiry Petrovich, the police inspector who interrogates Raskolnikov in *Crime and Punishment*, but one could also point to similarities between M'sieur Pierre and the character of Peter Petrovich Luzhin, a smug, self-satisfied man who seeks to marry Raskolnikov's sister; at one point in *Invitation to a Beheading*, Pierre is addressed as "Pyotr [Peter] Petrovich" (168/167). For a discussion of the Dostoevskian subtext, see Tammi, "Invitation to a Decoding. Dostoevskij as Subtext in Nabokov's *Priglašenie na kazn'*," *Scando-Slavica* 32 (1986): 51–72.

30. Nabokov, *Nikolai Gogol*, 73–74. One is also reminded of a character from Gogol's play *The Inspector General*. The town judge acknowledges that one of his officials constantly smells of vodka, but he goes on to say that the official claims he was dropped as a child and that ever since then he has given off the smell of vodka (see act 1, scene 1). Pierre informs Cincinnatus that his odor "runs in the family" and that he has been afflicted with it "since childhood" (146). For commentary on the connections between *Invitation to a Beheading* and Gogol's works, see Gavriel Shapiro's articles, "Reministsentsii iz 'Mertvykh dush' v 'Priglashenii na kazn'' Nabokova," *Gogolevskii*

sbornik, ed. S. A. Goncharov (St. Petersburg: Obrazovanie, 1994), 175–81; "Russkie literaturnye alliuzii v romane Nabokova *Priglashenie na kazn'*," *Russian Literature* 9 (1981): 369–78; and "Konflikt mezhdu protagonistom i okruzhaiushchim ego mirom v povesti N. V. Gogolia 'Shinel'' i v romane V. V. Nabokova *Priglashenie na kazn'*," *Russian Language Journal* 34, no. 119 (1980): 109–19.

31. Gavriel Shapiro argues that Pierre is a debased, parodic image of Satan. See "Khristianskie motivy, ikh ikonografiia i simvolika, v romane Vladimira Nabokova *Priglashenie na kazn'*," *Russian Language Journal* 33, no. 116 (1979): 148.

32. Varshavskii, *Nezamechennoe pokolenie*, 216.

33. Detailed discussions of these entities can be found in Guy Houk, "The Spider and the Moth: Nabokov's *Priglašenie na kazn'* as Epistemological Exhortation," *Russian Literature* 18 (1985): 31–41; and Gennady Barabtarlo, *Aerial View: Essays on Nabokov's Art and Metaphysics* (New York: Peter Lang, 1993), 21–37.

34. The spider is further linked to Pierre when it is characterized as "the youngest member of the circus family" (115/118). Pierre, of course, is both the ringleader and the main performer of the circus troupe.

35. Vladimir Nabokov, *The Stories of Vladimir Nabokov* (New York: Knopf, 1995), 136.

36. Her interaction with Cincinnatus ultimately supports Nabokov's subsequent remark that when Cincinnatus accuses his mother of being a parody, he is not being quite fair (see *SO*, 76).

37. See, e.g., G. M. Hyde, *Vladimir Nabokov: America's Russian Novelist* (London: Marion Boyars, 1977), 139.

38. The name of the gardens is itself significant. "Tamara" is also the name Nabokov gives to the figure of his first adolescent love in his autobiography *Speak, Memory* (see chapter 12); her real name was Valentina Shulgin. Phonetically, the name "Tamara" contains the seminal word *tam* – "there" – which plays such a significant role later in the novel as Cincinnatus tries to put into words his intuition of the existence of a better world somewhere out "there" (see the section "Language and Literature," above).

39. John M. Kopper, "The Prison in Nabokov's *Priglašenie*: A Place to Have the Time of One's Life," *Russian Language Journal* 41, no. 140 (1987): 177.

40. A further indication of the society's limited appreciation for the liter-

ary text is the fact that the prison library catalogue lists books not in alphabetical order but "according to the number of pages in each" (55)!

41. Alter, *"Invitation to a Beheading*: Nabokov and the Art of Politics," *TriQuarterly* 17 (1970): 54 (reprinted in the present volume). Alter also notes that the photographic orientation of the novel's point of view provides a further indication of its flawed premises. As he puts it, "[T]he art par excellence of this world of *poshlust* is photography," and he aptly points out how Pierre's artistic contribution, the "photohoroscope" of Emmie, is a "patently false contrivance, impotent to cope with the rich enigma of experience in time" (53–54).

42. It is also worth noting that Cincinnatus is to be beheaded on a chopping block made of oak – the very substance that serves as the focus of the society's most treasured novel. Cincinnatus's distinctive originality is to be sacrificed on the altar of spurious art.

43. The rhythms and spirit of Nabokov's prose here echo Charles Baudelaire's poem, "L'Invitation au voyage," which forms an important subtext for the novel (as noted in the articles by Alter and Peterson in the present volume).

44. For a detailed description of the Gnostic elements in *Invitation to a Beheading*, see Robert Grossmith's article, "Spiralizing the Circle," and Sergej Davydov's remarks on the novel in *The Garland Companion to Vladimir Nabokov* and in his monograph *"Teksty-Matreški" Vladimira Nabokova*.

45. See the article by Vladimir Alexandrov in the present volume and Brian Thomas Oles's comments in his article, "Silence and the Ineffable in Nabokov's *Invitation to a Beheading*," *Nabokov Studies* 2 (1995): 202–3. Nabokov himself remained guarded when commenting on his personal beliefs. Characteristic is this reply to an interviewer's question about whether he believed in God: "To be quite candid – and what I am going to say now is something I never said before, and I hope it provokes a salutory little chill – I know more than I can express in words, and the little I can express would not have been expressed, had I not known more" (*SO*, 45). He did affirm, however, that "philosophically" he was an "indivisible monist" (*SO*, 85; cf. *SO*, 124).

46. This reference to "schooling" anticipates the end of the chapter, when Cincinnatus recalls the day he first "learned how to make letters" and had joined the children who "knew how to copy the model words from the flower beds in the school garden" (96/101). That day was memorable, for it

was also the day he realized he was different from the others and perhaps even had the ability to walk on air (96–97/102)! It was presumably from this day on that he began to conceal his difference and thus to obscure his unique, inner knowledge with the conventional, ready-made words of his schoolmasters.

47. Gavriel Shapiro has identified the "ancient poem" as Mikhail Lermontov's "The Neighbor Girl" ("Sosedka"); see "Russkie literaturnye alliuzii," 370.

48. Two examples of such misguided "plagiarism" are the characters of Anton Petrovich in "An Affair of Honor" ("Podlets") and the narrator Smurov in *The Eye*. For a discussion of this recurring theme in Nabokov's work, see Julian Connolly, *Nabokov's Early Fiction: Patterns of Self and Other* (Cambridge: Cambridge University Press, 1992), 48–51, 108–11. It may also be worth noting that Emmie's name could point to another unfaithful literary character – the heroine of Flaubert's *Madame Bovary*; see Guy Houk, "The Spider and the Moth," 33. That Emmie would ultimately prove to be a false savior is signaled early in the novel when Cincinnatus hears a tapping noise like that of "an invisible woodpecker" (75/82). Hearing in this sound an "invitation," Cincinnatus discovers that it is produced by Emmie bouncing a ball against a prison wall. Just a short time later, however, Cincinnatus sees Pierre tacking up a calendar in his cell: "tap, tap, like a woodpecker" (78/85). Emmie and Pierre are thus linked together.

49. Some readers have found an affinity between Cincinnatus's emergence from a crumbling, artificial world and Alice's rebellion against the pack of cards near the end of *Alice in Wonderland*. See, e.g., Gleb Struve, "Notes on Nabokov as a Russian Writer," in *Nabokov: The Man and His Work*, ed. L. S. Dembo (Madison: University of Wisconsin Press, 1967), 48. Nabokov had translated (and Russified) *Alice in Wonderland* in 1921. For a description of this translation, see Julian Connolly, *"Ania v strane chudes,"* in *The Garland Companion to Vladimir Nabokov*, 18–25.

50. Davydov, *"Invitation to a Beheading,"* *The Garland Companion to Vladimir Nabokov*, 194.

51. See Shapiro, "Khristianskie motivy," 144.

52. Pekka Tammi writes that the entire scene "is couched to suggest the archetypal ascension of Christ after his sufferings were over"; see "Invitation to a Decoding," 69. Nora Buhks, on the other hand, points out that Cincinnatus himself does not see in his life any messianic significance; see Buhks,

"Eshafot v khrustal'nom dvortse. O romane Vl. Nabokova *Priglashenie na kazn'*," *Cahiers du Monde russe* 35.4 (1994): 828. Any similarities between Cincinnatus's experience and that of Jesus Christ would underscore Cincinnatus's status as a martyr, not as a divinity.

53. See, for example, Osip Mandelstam's poem of 1920, "In Petersburg we shall meet again" ("V Peterburge my soidemsia snova").

54. For an excellent account of Nabokov's family background and upbringing, see Brian Boyd, *Vladimir Nabokov: The Russian Years* (Princeton, N.J.: Princeton University Press, 1990).

55. See Boyd, *The Russian Years*, 79, 91–95; see also *SO*, 42–43.

56. Nabokov's admiration for Kafka's *Metamorphosis* has encouraged some critics to identify parallels between *Invitation to a Beheading* and Kafka's *The Castle* and *The Trial*; see Margaret Byrd Boegeman, "*Invitation to a Beheading* and the Many Shades of Kafka," in *Nabokov's Fifth Arc: Nabokov and Others on His Life's Work*, ed. J. E. Rivers and Charles Nicol (Austin: University of Texas Press, 1982), 105–21. Nabokov himself denied any influence of (and familiarity with) these works at the time of *Invitation's* creation, and several critics have remarked on the stark contrast between the guilt-ridden atmosphere of Kafka's work and the ultimately triumphant spirit that emerges in Nabokov's novel. See, e.g., Rampton, *Vladimir Nabokov*, 60–61. John Burt Foster provides a succinct analysis of Nabokov's attitude toward Kafka in his essay "Nabokov and Kafka" in *The Garland Companion to Vladimir Nabokov*, 444–51.

57. For a discussion of the way this work anticipates and contrasts with *Invitation to a Beheading*, see Julian Connolly, "Nabokov's 'Terra Incognita' and 'Invitation to a Beheading': The Struggle for Imaginative Freedom," *Wiener Slawistischer Almanach* 12 (1983): 55–65.

58. See Vladimir Nabokov, *Pale Fire* (New York: G. P. Putnam's Sons, 1962), 238. The comment is made by the poet John Shade who corrects a woman who has called another individual a "loony": Shade affirms that this fellow is "a fellow poet."

59. Nabokov, *The Stories of Vladimir Nabokov*, 463.

60. Ibid., 461.

61. Ibid.

62. Nabokov, *Speak, Memory* (New York: G. P. Putnam's Sons, 1966), 297; emphasis added.

63. For the details of this tragedy, see Boyd, *Vladimir Nabokov: The Russian Years*, 189–193.

64. Vladimir Nabokov, *Poems and Problems* (New York: McGraw-Hill, 1981), 73.

65. Vladimir Nabokov, *The Gift*, trans. Michael Scammell with the author's collaboration (New York: G. P. Putnam's Sons, 1963), 215. Nabokov's own father was a vigorous opponent of the death penalty; see Boyd, *Vladimir Nabokov: The Russian Years*, 33–34.

66. Alexander Dolinin provides an apt description of the relationship between *The Gift* and *Invitation to a Beheading*: "To a certain extent, the predicament of Cincinnatus C. mimics and heightens that of Chernyshevski, turning the farcical into the tragic, and vice versa" (see his essay on *The Gift* in *The Garland Companion to Vladimir Nabokov*, 136–37).

67. Additional points of correspondence between *The Gift* and *Invitation to a Beheading* are discussed by Brian Boyd in *Vladimir Nabokov: The Russian Years*, 416–17, and by Nora Buhks in "Eshafot v khrustal'nom dvortse," 821–38.

68. See D. Barton Johnson, *Worlds in Regression: Some Novels of Vladimir Nabokov* (Ann Arbor, Mich.: Ardis, 1985), 99. Gavriel Shapiro points out that the name Delaland may derive from the French astronomer Joseph Jérôme Le Français de Lalande (1732–1807) whom Nabokov mentions in his commentary to *Eugene Onegin* (see Shapiro, "Russkie literaturnye alliuzii," 369).

69. This is the position Gennady Barabtarlo takes; see his *Aerial View*, 32.

70. Nabokov would leave Germany for good in 1937. In 1940 he emigrated to the United States and later adopted U.S. citizenship. After the success of *Lolita* in the late 1950s Nabokov moved back to Europe with his wife. Eventually he settled in Montreux, Switzerland, where he died in 1977.

71. This work has particular affinities with *Invitation to a Beheading* in that the beginning of the story depicts the created world being assembled for the creative consciousness, and the ending shows it being dispersed again. For a discussion of the relationship between the short story and the novel, see Connolly, *Nabokov's Early Fiction*, 161–66.

72. Nabokov, *The Stories of Vladimir Nabokov*, 432. Like Cincinnatus, this protagonist has had a glimpse of an "otherworld" of unutterable beauty: it is for that realm that he wishes to be released from the mundane world around him. At the end of the tale, the narrator "let him go" (433).

73. Vladimir Nabokov, *Bend Sinister* (New York: McGraw-Hill, 1974), 241.

74. Dale Peterson discusses this type of reader response to the novel and shows why such a response is ultimately one-sided and limited (see his article in the present volume).

75. Leona Toker, *Nabokov: The Mystery of Literary Structure* (Ithaca, N.Y.: Cornell University Press, 1989), 127. A remark that Nabokov made in a letter to his sister in 1946 offers illumination in this regard: "My darling, no matter how much one wants to hide in one's ivory tower, there are things that wound one too deeply: for example, German atrocities, the burning of children in ovens – children who are just as ravishingly amusing and beloved as our own. I retreat into myself, but there I find such hatred toward the Germans, toward the concentration camps, toward every kind of tyranny, that, as a refuge, ce n'est pas grand'chose" (Vladimir Nabokov, *Perepiska s sestroi* [Ann Arbor, Mich.: Ardis, 1985], 41; the translation is mine).

II  CRITICISM

Invitation to a Beheading: Nabokov and the Art of Politics

ROBERT ALTER

The logical result of Fascism is the introduction of aesthetics into politics. . . . Mankind's self-alienation has reached such a degree that it can experience its own destruction as an aesthetic pleasure of the first order.

    —Walter Benjamin, "The Work of Art in the Age of Mechanical Reproduction"

Because *Invitation to a Beheading* is in many ways the most explicit of Nabokov's fictions of ostentatious artifice, it at once lucidly illustrates his conception of the novel and puts to the test the limits of that conception. Over the past few years, with the publication in English of most of Nabokov's Russian fiction, and with a growing body of intelligent American criticism on his novels, the brilliance of his technical virtuosity has come to be widely appreciated, but a suspicion persists in some critical circles that his achievement is mere technical virtuosity, that the intricately convoluted designs of his novels make them self-enclosed, sterile, and therefore finally "minor." What is at issue is not just a critical commitment to realism – a literary convention toward which Nabokov has shown both lofty disdain and impish mockery – but an expectation of moral seriousness in literature that goes back in English criticism to figures like Matthew Arnold and Samuel Johnson. For American and British critics deriving from this tradition, the novel, though it may and perhaps even should delight, must above all teach us something – about the social, political, and spiritual spheres we inhabit, about the nature of moral choice and character, about the complexities of our psychological makeup. The obviously centripetal direction, then, of Nabokov's imagination, whirling all social, political, and psychological materials into a circumscribed inner concern with art and the artist, is construed as the novelist's failure to engage the larger world of human experience and would seem to confess his ultimate lack of seriousness. *Invitation to a Beheading* is surely an extreme instance of this general centripetal movement. Written in Berlin in 1935, it takes the ugliest, most disturbing of modern political actualities, the totalitarian state, and uses it, one gathers, merely as a dramatically convenient background for the recurrent Nabokovian theme, which is, to borrow Simon Karlinsky's apt formulation, "the nature of the creative imagination and the solitary, freak-like role into which a man gifted with such imagination is inevitably cast in any society."[1]

The narrator of *Invitation to a Beheading* plays so continually and conspicuously with the status of his narration as artifice that the general point hardly needs critical elaboration. The first paragraph of the novel informs us that the protagonist has been sentenced to die, and immediately the narrator pauses to remind us that we are reading a book, and a rather peculiar one, at that: "So we are nearing the end. The right-hand, still untasted part of the novel . . . has suddenly, for no reason at all, become quite meager: a few minutes of quick reading, already downhill, and – O horrible!"[2] In the conventional novel of imprisonment, in the conventional fictional pattern of crime and punishment, the sentencing of the hero would of course take place toward the end, after a long and arduous development, so we are put on notice at once that conventional expectations will be subverted in the particular fiction before us. As we move on, Nabokov takes pains to remind us repeatedly that each scene has been arranged by a theatrical stage manager: again and again, visual descriptions are conveyed in explicitly painterly terms, even made to seem two-dimensional painted backdrops; if there is an atmospheric disturbance, it has to be reported as "a summer thunderstorm, simply yet tastefully staged, . . . performed outside" (129); time itself, as Cincinnatus points out, is not a continuous flow, like time in the "real" world, but purely a series of conventional indications within a represented action: "[N]ote the clock in the corridor. The dial is blank; however, every hour the watchman washes off the old hand and daubs on a new one – and that's how we live, by tarbrush time" (135). And so the novel proceeds, through dozens of ingenious variations on this one underlying idea down to the grand finale when the daubed-in perspective slips out of kilter, the scenery totters, the painted rows of spectators come crashing down, and Cincinnatus goes striding off toward what we hope is a more human world.

All this flaunted artifice is clear enough in the novel, and it makes good thematic sense in relation to the hero, whose unspeakable sin of "gnostic turpitude" consists, after all, in imagining the world as an artist and in wanting to become what the world he exists in cannot by its nature tolerate, a true writer. It is precisely this continuous concern, however, with the artist's predicament that the devotees of high seriousness object to in Nabokov. Has the writer not shirked his responsibilities by converting totalitarianism into the stuff of a fable about art and artifice? Can there be anything but frivolous self-indulgence in his decision finally to collapse the totalitarian state into mere discarded stage machinery, at the very moment in history when all civilized values were threatened by Stalinist terror and Nazi bestiality?

Such objections, it seems to me, conceive in far too narrow terms the ways in which fiction may "engage the world of experience" or are predicated on rather restrictive notions of what is involved in experience – even political experience. I would argue, on the contrary, that an important inner connection exists between the special emphasis on ostentatious artifice in *Invitation to a Beheading* and the totalitarian world that is the setting of the novel. I would argue, too, that Nabokov, precisely through his concern for art and the fate of the artist, is able to illuminate a central aspect of the supposedly human condition in an era of police states and totalitarian terrors. Two years after writing *Invitation to a Beheading*, Nabokov included in *The Gift* a kind of meditation about the meaning of executions, which could serve as a useful gloss on the entire nature of political and social reality in the earlier novel:

Fyodor recalled his father saying that innate in every man is the feeling of something insuperably abnormal about the death penalty, something like the uncanny reversal of action in a looking glass that makes everyone left-handed: not for nothing is everything reversed for the executioner: the horse-collar is put on upside down when the robber Razin is taken to the scaffold; wine is poured for the headsman not with a natural turn of the wrist but backhandedly; and if, according to the Swabian code, an insulted actor was permitted to seek satisfaction by striking the *shadow* of the offender, in China it was precisely an actor – a shadow – who fulfilled the duties of the executioner, all responsibility being as it were lifted from the world of men and transformed into the inside-out one of mirrors.[3]

Now, in order to make sense of this seemingly fanciful notion, we shall have to raise the tactless question of what, in fact, Nabokov conceives reality to be. This would appear to be particularly foolish to ask of a writer who has warned that reality is a word never to be used except within quotation marks, but I believe it is of the utmost relevance to Nabokov's whole literary enterprise, the ultimate concerns of which are epistemological and metaphysical – like those of his great English precursor in the fiction of ostentatious artifice, Laurence Sterne. Nabokov, like Sterne, is continually bemused by the mystery through which individual consciousness in a subtle and at times perverse alchemic process transmutes the brute data of experience into the "reality" which each of us inhabits. The key to any sense of reality, certainly for Nabokov and probably for all of us, is the perception of pattern. Consciousness needs at least the illusion that it can control some of the data it encounters, seeing in them orderly sequence, recurrence, analogy, cause and effect, to be able to believe in their reality: the sun sets, the sun also rises, says the preacher, but if it never rose again, if it came up as a thousand incandescent fireballs or a great gleaming poppyseed cake, we would be in a nightmare or a fun-house fantasy, not in what most of us would call the real world. For Nabokov, as consciousness achieves a condition of acrobatic poise and elastic strength, integrating more and more into meaningful patterns, it encounters more reality, or rather makes the world around it at last real. That is why Cincinnatus, trapped in a world that he repeatedly reminds us is a mad jumble of "senseless visions, bad dreams, dregs of delirium; the drivel of nightmares" (36), is not an escapist but a defiant rebel when he envisages another existence comprised of perfect, endlessly delighting pattern: "*There, tam, là-bas*, the gaze of men glows with inimitable understanding; *there* the freaks that are tortured here walk unmolested; *there* time takes shape according to one's pleasure, like a figured rug whose folds can be gathered in such a way that two designs will meet" (94). The most prominent literary echo here is of course Baudelaire's vision of perfected art and pleasure in "L'Invitation au voyage" – "*Là, tout n'est qu'ordre et beauté, / Luxe, calme et volupté*" (There, all is pure order and beauty, / Sumptuousness, calm, and pleasure) – while those artfully gathered folds of patterned time nicely characterize Nabokov's subsequent treatment of time in *Speak, Memory*, his attempt to fix through art the reality of his personal experience. What may seem peculiar is the obtrusion into Cincinnatus's vision of aesthetic bliss of an explicitly moral idea, that in the harmonious world elsewhere the poor tormented freaks of his own flawed world will be left unharmed. To begin to understand this interweaving of the moral and the aesthetic, we must return to the shadowy headsman of Fyodor's father's reflections, who stands still unexplained in his backhanded, inside-out realm of mirrors.

If consciousness is the medium through which reality comes into being, the sudden and final obliteration of consciousness through mechanical means is the supreme affirmation by human agents – the executioners – of the principle of irreality. For the mind's ability to perceive freely or create patterns and delight in them is what makes man's life human, but in the appointed executioner mind is focused down to guiding the motions that will blot out all pattern in another human mind, man in a grim farce pretending that he is not a sentient being but something like a falling tree or an avalanche, a stupid instrument of blind murderous forces. Execution is the central rite of

Cincinnatus's world, realizing its utmost possibilities, because that world, in all its institutional arrangements and daily social relations, is explicitly contrived to numb, cloud, cripple, and finally extirpate individual consciousness. It therefore must remain a relentlessly incredible world from the viewpoint of any genuinely human consciousness – its halls filled with trick mirrors producing meretricious effects, its personages crudely painted clowns more papier-mâché than flesh, even the conventional spider in its prison cell turning out to be a rubber facsimile, the shoddy practical joke of a dime-store mentality. Here, as elsewhere, Nabokov's antirealist method has the effect of probing to the roots of real experience: his totalitarian state is not in any sense a disguised description of an actual regime, but the lineaments of his fictional fantasy, drawn with a rigorous sense of self-consistency (and not freely improvised like the fictions of some fashionable American "fantasts"), revealing the ultimate implications of the totalitarian principle and constituting a kind of ideal model of totalitarian possibilities. Thus one critic could, with considerable justice, see in this novel a prophetic insight into the underlying operative assumption in Hitler's enterprise of mass-manufactured death: "the unspoken, vile, dehumanizing assumption that the guiltless victim must collaborate in his own torture and death, must enter into the corruption of his tormentors and depart this world robbed of life, integrity and individuality alike."[4] What must be added is that this world of ultimate obscenity is deliberately, justifiably, held at a comic distance so that the horror does not overwhelm, so that the whole insidious mechanism can be examined by a humane critical intelligence that affirms its own power to prevail through its constant presence in the cunning concern of the narrator for the embattled humanity of his protagonist. If the observer is able to preserve an intelligent sense of the possibilities of consciousness, then a society based on a universal collusion to surrender consciousness must seem to him a grotesque and improbable farce, a congeries of "specters, werewolves, parodies" (40) that is sinister in both senses of the word – menacing and belonging to a left-handed, inverted realm of mere negation.

It is worth examining more closely the relation between the theme of art in the foreground and the political background of the novel. Sartre's dictum that "a novelist's aesthetic always sends us back to his metaphysic" is eminently applicable here, and I think it is also relevant to keep in mind Sartre's rather special sense of "metaphysic," which implies not merely a conceptual grasp of reality but a moral posture toward it. Even what seems to be a preoccupation with the mechanics of technique on Nabokov's part has a strict thematic function, and this is especially true of a recurrent peculiarity of *Invitation to a Beheading* – that so many of its scenes are conceived as formal exercises in vision. Here, for example, is a brief description of the prisoner futilely attempting to see out of his cell window:

> Cincinnatus was standing on tiptoe, holding the iron bars with his small hands, which were all white from the strain, and half of his face was covered with a sunny grating, and the gold of his left mustache shone, and there was a tiny golden cage in each of his mirrorlike pupils, while below, from behind, his heels rose out of the too-large slippers. (29)

The physical image of Cincinnatus is of course sharply and meticulously defined, made to seem very "real" – and not only the physical image, because through that final, telling detail of the oversize slippers we get a sense of the sad, touching, pathetic, vaguely funny nature of this trapped figure. What is important to note is that virtually every phrase of the description makes us aware of the cunning artificer, framing, selecting, eliciting pattern. Nabokov in effect invites us to participate in the perception of how a painter (a Flemish realist, let us say) and, by implication, a novelist, goes about "realizing" a scene. Each of the minute details, the small hands white with gripping, the gleaming half-mustache, the bars reflected in the pupils, is strategically chosen to make us see the whole figure caught in a particular light and a particular posture. We are led simultaneously to envisage Cincinnatus as a human being in a moment of anguish and as a formal study in dark and light contrasts, symmetrically divided by shadow. The reflecting surface is of course an invaluable resource in such studies of the possibilities of representation – one recalls the mirrors in Van Eyck interiors – because it allows the artist to duplicate forms and objects on a different scale, from a different angle, or even to smuggle new presences into the scene. The golden cages, however, in Cincinnatus's eyes are more than a device of visual preciosity, for in our very awareness of their paradoxical beauty we are led back to the terror of Cincinnatus's entrapment. Is the cage in fact inside his head, a function of his own mode of vision, or, alternately, has an actual imprisonment cut him off from reality, reducing vision to an infinite regress of unyielding bars, so that, as for Rilke's caged panther, *"Ihm ist, als ob es tausend Stäbe gäbe, / Und hinter tausend Stäben keine Welt"* (For him, it's as though there were a thousand bars / And behind a thousand bars no world)?

Let us look at another, more elaborate instance of these exercises in vision. Cincinnatus frequently thinks back to the shreds of happiness he was able to grasp in the Tamara Gardens; it is the one place in which he can imagine concretely something like a human environment. But it should be noted that even in nostalgia he does not simply recall the Gardens, he explicitly envisages them. At one point he is brought out by his captors onto the turret of the prison and looks down on the town below:

> Our travelers found themselves on a broad terrace at the top of a tower, whence there was a breathtaking view, since not only was the tower huge, but the whole fortress towered hugely on the crest of a huge cliff, of which it seemed to be a monstrous outgrowth. Far below one could see the almost vertical vineyards, and the creamy road that wound down to the dry river bed; a tiny person in red was crossing the convex bridge; the speck running in front of him was most likely a dog.
>
> Further away the sun-flooded town described an ample hemicycle: some of the varicolored houses proceeded in even rows, accompanied by round trees, while others, awry, crept down slopes, stepping on their own shadows; one could distinguish the

traffic moving on First Boulevard, and an amethystine shimmer at the end, where the famous fountain played; and still further, toward the hazy folds of the hills that formed the horizon, there was the dark stipple of oak groves, with, here and there, a pond gleaming like a hand mirror, while other bright ovals of water gathered, glowing through the tender mist, over there to the west, where the serpentine Strop had its source. Cincinnatus, his palm pressed to his cheek, in motionless, ineffably vague and perhaps even blissful despair, gazed at the glimmer and haze of the Tamara Gardens and at the dove-blue melting hills beyond them – oh, it was a long time before he could take his eyes away. (42–43)

If the passage demonstrates a rigorous adherence to consistent point of view, it is point of view more in the sense of a Brueghel than a Henry James. The paradoxical effectiveness of the description, like that of Cincinnatus clinging to the bars, depends on our awareness that the scene seems real precisely because it is a scrupulously ordered artistic composition. As we look down on the scene with Cincinnatus, we are taken into the magic of its presence by being made to see it as a painting. The foreground is defined, in a painterly repetition of form, as a duplication in outline with diminished scale – a huge tower on a fortress towering hugely on a cliff. The eye is then led down through the most careful arrangement of perspective along the winding road (formally duplicated further down in the serpentine line of the river), past the tiny human figure on the convex bridge and the indistinguishable speck which is "most likely a dog," on to the town itself and the bluish haze of the hills at the horizon. Effects of color and light are nicely balanced in painterly fashion and conveyed to us in a vocabulary that suggests the artist's nuanced choice of pigments and even something of the way he applies them to his canvas: We move from the "creamy" road to the red figure, then into the "sun-flooded" town with its "varicolored" houses, set off by the "hazy folds of the hills" in the distance and the "dark stipple" of the woods just below the hills. The vocabulary of color is not only precise in its distinctions but also designed to communicate a sense of the pleasure – an almost sensual delight in the opulence of beauty – that informs aesthetic experience. This is why the road is "creamy," the distant fountain an "amethystine shimmer" in the sunlight, the horizon an inviting vision of "dove-blue melting hills." Inevitably there are reflecting surfaces in the picture, those ponds seen gleaming like hand mirrors in the park far below, the mirror here serving the rather simple function of illustrating the artist's exquisite ordering of effects of light and perspective in the scene. Finally, there is one detail in the landscape that goes beyond the decorum of painterly terms, the houses creeping down the slope, "stepping on their own shadows." The graphic personification, however, seems perfectly right because it suggests how a scene done with painstaking art begins to transcend the limits of its own medium, assuming an elusive life that is more than color and line, plane and texture.

Such passages offer ample evidence of Nabokov's virtuosity, but looking at them, as we have so far, out of context, we have not yet answered the question of what it is all for. These scenes actually stand in a relation of dialectic tension to the world of the novel in which they occur, and one clear indication of that is the artful placement of mirrors within them. Fyodor's father, we recall, uses mirrors in a negative sense, connecting them with death and irreality, but in *Invitation to a Beheading* there are good and bad uses of mirrors, just as there is good and bad art. Nabokov invokes a whole spectrum of traditional symbolic associations suggested by mirrors – the mirror of art held to nature; the mirror of consciousness "reflecting" reality (or does it only reflect itself, we are at least led to wonder; is Cincinnatus's prison merely a house of mirrors?); the mirror as a depthless, inverted, unreal, mocking imitation of the real world. The most striking development of the mirror idea in the novel is appropriately ambiguous, Nabokov's memorable parable of imagination and reality, the crazily rippled "*nonnon mirrors*" which, when set opposite complementarily shapeless lumps, reflect beautifully "real" forms, the two negatives making a positive. Is this a model for the alchemy that the imagination works on formless reality, or does it rather illustrate the kind of mountebank's trick that has come to serve as a manufactured substitute for art, a merely illusionistic amusement for the masses? The former alternative, in which one can see the distorted magical mirrors as an image of Nabokov's own art, is clearly the more attractive of the two, but the fact that the device of the *nonnons* is reported to us by Cincinnatus's mother, herself the tricky insubstantial creature of a dimensionless world, at any rate leaves a teasing residue of doubt in our minds.

Elsewhere in the novel, the contexts in which mirrors appear are more clearly negative. For the insidious M'sieur Pierre, they are the implements of a self-admiring, self-absorbed hedonism: "[T]here is nothing more pleasant," he tells Cincinnatus, laying claim to a background of subtle sexual expertise, "than to surround oneself with mirrors and watch the good work going on there" (145). For Marthe, Cincinnatus's inexhaustibly promiscuous wife, the mirror is the most patently fake stage prop in her factitious world of theatrical (or rather farcical) deceptions. As part of the domestic scenery that she has temporarily moved into Cincinnatus's cell, "[t]here came a mirrored wardrobe, bringing with it its own private reflection (namely, a corner of the connubial bedroom with a stripe of sunlight across the floor, a dropped glove, and an open door in the distance)" (99). More ambiguously, Cincinnatus himself adopts the tricky role of the mirror as a stratagem of survival. A mirror is of course a transparent surface with an opaque backing, and Cincinnatus, an opaque figure in a world of mutually transparent souls, learns to "feign translucence, employing a complex system of optical illusions, as it were" (24), that is, reflecting to those around him a fleeting simulacrum of translucence from the surface of his immutable opacity.

It is precisely the association of mirrors with both art and consciousness that justifies this range of ambiguities in their appearance in the novel. For while Cincinnatus dreams of, and at certain moments his creator pointedly exercises, a beautifully patterned art, the most essential quality of the world that imprisons him is cheap, false, meretricious, mechanical art. More succinctly, Nabokov's ideal model of the totalitarian state is, to invoke the embracing Russian term he explains so elaborately in his study of Gogol, a world of *poshlust*. The leering, inane faces of *poshlust* are everywhere in *Invitation to a Beheading*, but I will try briefly to review some of the most symptomatic instances. The act of murder by state decree is imagined by its perpetrators as a work of art. M'sieur Pierre fancies himself an *artiste*, carrying his headsman's axe in a velvet-lined case like a musical instrument. In his person and manner M'sieur Pierre is obviously the embodiment of quintessential *poshlust*, often with excruciating detail, as in the two illusionistic green leaves he has tattooed around his left nipple to make it seem "a rosebud . . . of marchpane and candied angelica" (160). The eve of Cincinnatus's execution is marked by a grandiose ceremony that smacks of a crucifixion staged in Radio City Music Hall with a thousand dancing Rockettes. A million varicolored light bulbs are planted "artfully" (the narrator's word) in the grass to form a monogram of the initials of the headsman and his victim. The chief ingredients of this "art" are monstrous quantity and mechanical means; appropriately, the production is sloppily arranged and does not quite come off.

Bad art, in fact, is the ubiquitous instrument of torture for the imprisoned Cincinnatus. Thus in a niche in the prison corridor, he sees what he imagines is a window through which he will be able to look down on the longed-for Tamara Gardens in the town below, but when he approaches he discovers that it is a crude trompe l'oeil painting: "This landscape, daubed in several layers of distance, executed in blurry green hues and illuminated by concealed bulbs, was reminiscent . . . of the backdrop in front of which a wind orchestra toils and puffs" (76). The colors are drab, the treetops stirless, the lighting torpid, in short the painting is in every respect the exact opposite of that artfully composed view of the town and the Gardens that Cincinnatus had enjoyed earlier from the prison tower.

The use of hidden light bulbs as part of an unconvincingly illusionistic effect is significant because the substitution of mechanical device for imagination is the key to most of the bad art in the novel. Thus the art par excellence of this world of *poshlust* is photography. It is essential to the grand production on the eve of the beheading that Cincinnatus and his executioner be photographed together by flashbulb light (predictably, with hideous results). At the beginning of the novel, the prisoner is brought the two local newspapers with two weirdly complementary color photographs of his house on the front page (and one should keep in mind, of course, the inevitably false, blurry, bleeding quality of color photographs reproduced on newsprint). One picture shows the facade of the house, with the photographer from the second paper peering out of Marthe's bedroom window. The other, taken from that window, shows the garden and gate with the first photographer shooting the facade of the house. The circularity of the two photographs is just the reverse of Nabokov's practice of introducing hints of his own presence as artificer into his fictions. Here each of the photographers is inadvertently caught by the other in the act of using his mechanical black box to snap the scene, and the tawdry nature of the whole procedure is emphasized by the clear hint of still another sexual betrayal by Marthe in the presence of the photographer in her bedroom (23).

The culminating example of the mechanical art of photograhy as the instrument of *poshlust* is the "photohoroscope" devised by M'sieur Pierre. Using retouched snapshots of Emmie, the warden's young daughter, placing her face in montage with photographs of older people in other circumstances, he offers a chronological record of a hypothetical woman's life, from childhood to old age and death (167–71). The simulation of a life is of course utterly unconvincing, and there is something vaguely obscene about this face of a little girl faked up as the face of a mature woman and then of an old lady. The photohoroscope is an ultimate achievement of anti-art, using purely mechanical means to produce a patently false contrivance, impotent to cope with the rich enigma of experience in time, blind to the dimension of consciousness, profaning the mystery of human life. The companion piece to M'sieur Pierre's album is the novel *Quercus* that Cincinnatus takes out of the prison library. This three-thousand-page tome on the life of an oak tree, "considered to be the acme of modern thought," is Nabokov's reductio ad absurdum of the naturalistic novel and of the principle of exhaustive documentary realism:

> It seemed as though the author were sitting with his camera somewhere among the topmost branches of the Quercus, spying out and catching his prey. Various images of life would come and go, pausing among the green macules of light. The normal periods of inaction were filled with scientific descriptions of the oak itself, from the viewpoints of dendrology, ornithology, coleopterology, mythology – or popular descriptions, with touches of folk humor. (123)

Such photographic realism, in other words, is mindless, formless, pointless, infinitely tedious, devoid of humanity. It denies imagination, spontaneity, the shaping power of human consciousness; subverting everything art should be, it produces the perfect novel of a totalitarian world.

At this point seekers of high seriousness might be moved to object: a merely *aesthetic* critique of totalitarianism, an objection to it on the grounds of its bad taste? This novel does offer an aesthetic critique of the totalitarian idea, but it is not "merely" that because art implies so much more than good taste for Nabokov. As I shall now try to make clear, Nabokov's aesthetic in fact leads us back to a metaphysic, and one with ultimately moral implications. In his discussion of *poshlust* apropos of *Dead Souls*, Nabokov remarks parenthetically that it is a quality "which yawns universally at times of revolution or war."[5] I am tempted to see a Popean pun in "yawns," like the great apocalyptic pun near the end of the *Dunciad* in which Dulness yawns – both announcing the soporific reign of universal tedium and threatening to engulf civilization. In any case, the world of Pope's Dunciad offers a suggestive analogy to that of *Invitation to a Beheading*, being a hilarious yet ominous farce that represents a general breakdown of humanistic values, where the intellect is put to such widespread perverted use that art and thinking become impossible. What needs emphasis, however, is that Nabokov notes the prevalence of *poshlust* under conditions of political absolutism not merely because it is an observable and offensive aspect of revolutionary and militant regimes – from Stalinist statuary to Mussolinian murals – but because he recognizes in it an indispensable principle of such regimes, a necessary expression of their inner nature.

If we look across from literature to the evidence of history, the gratuitous gestures of the totalitarian state may provide us a clue precisely because they are made out of inner necessity, not from the need to achieve practical ends. Thus it was the compulsion of their moving spirit, not real utility, that led the Nazis to welcome their unspeakable trainloads of doomed human cattle with brass bands at the railroad sidings blaring cheery patriotic songs. This is totalitarian *poshlust* in the purest form of its moral and aesthetic obscenity; it takes little effort to imagine M'sieur Pierre waving the baton for such a grisly band, a vaguely beery smile playing over his lips. *Poshlust* is indispensable to totalitarianism because it is the natural expression of a deadened consciousness persuaded it is devoted to lofty ends, and at the same time it is the means of foisting sham values, anesthetizing still human imaginations until they are incapable of making sane distinctions: ugly becomes beautiful, death becomes life, and over the portals of a man-made hell one affixes an ostensibly noble sentiment like *Arbeit macht frei*. "Sentimentality," Norman Mailer has written, "is the emotional promiscuity of those who have no sentiment"; this is why it is in a hideously trashy sentimentalism that the totalitarian spirit comes to full, festering florescence.

There is one passage in *Invitation to a Beheading* that finely illuminates this whole question of the essential, inexorable antagonism between totalitarianism and authentic art. It provides an especially forceful example of how art for Nabokov is inevitably connected with a larger vision of man because here he also deals with the limits of art. We are observing Cincinnatus in his cell once more, though from whose viewpoint we are not informed until the sudden, unsettling turn near the end of the paragraph. Again, we are given a portrait composed of precisely selected details – the texture of his skin and hair, the state of his clothing, the movement of his eyes –

with abundant indications that these are the details of a carefully
executed painting. All these minute particulars, we are told, "completed a picture" that was made up

> of a thousand barely noticeable, overlapping trifles: of the light
> outline of his lips, seemingly not quite fully drawn but touched by
> a master of masters; of the fluttering movements of his empty,
> not-yet-shaded-in hands; of the dispersing and again gathering
> rays in his animated eyes; but even all of this, analyzed and stud-
> ied, still could not fully explain Cincinnatus: it was as if one side of
> his being slid into another dimenson, as all the complexity of a
> tree's foliage passes from shade into radiance, so that you cannot
> distinguish just where begins the submergence into the shimmer
> of a different element. It seemed as though at any moment, in the
> course of his movements about the limited space of the haphaz-
> ardly invented cell, Cincinnatus would step in such a way as to slip
> naturally and effortlessly through some chink of the air into its
> unknown coulisses to disappear there with the same easy smooth-
> ness with which the reflection of a rotated mirror moves across
> every object in the room and suddenly vanishes, as if beyond the
> air, in some new depth of ether. At the same time, everything
> about him breathed with a delicate, drowsy, but in reality excep-
> tionally strong, ardent and independent life: his veins of the bluest
> blue pulsated; crystal-clear saliva moistened his lips; the skin quiv-
> ered on his cheeks and his forehead, which was edged with dis-
> solved light . . . and all this so teased the observer as to make him
> long to tear apart, cut to shreds, destroy utterly this brazen elusive
> flesh, and all that it implied and expressed, all that impossible,
> dazzling freedom – enough, enough – do not walk any more,
> Cincinnatus, lie down on your cot, so you will not arouse, will not
> irritate . . . And in truth Cincinnatus would become aware of the
> predatory eye in the peephole following him and lie down or sit at
> the table and open a book. (121–22)

The opposing attitudes toward human life of the artist and the
totalitarian are beautifully dramatized in the contrasted responses to

ultimate frustration of the painter's eye at the beginning of the passage and the jailer's eye at the end. Elsewhere in the novel, we have seen how the cunning artist celebrates the power of art to fix reality in arresting pattern; here, however, the narrator confesses the final impotence-in-power of art before the stubborn mystery of an individual human life. In other passages, we noted the use of mirrors as reflecting and perspectivistic devices that demonstrated the magisterial control of the artist over his materials; here, by contrast, there is no actual mirror in the scene: instead, the mirror is introduced as a simile, a fragment of visual experience used figuratively with paradoxical effectiveness to define the limits of visual representation. Partial readings of Nabokov's novels have sometimes led to the inference that the world they portray is fundamentally a world of aesthetic solipsism, but this passage makes clear that it is life rather than art alone that is inexhaustible, and that art's ability to renew itself, to be infinitely various and captivating, finally depends on its necessary inadequacy in the face of the inexhaustible enigma of conscious life. The artist's human subject here glimmers, shimmers, slides into a hidden dimension beyond visualization, but the very frustration of the artist's purpose brings him back to his subject with a sense of loving wonder – all that ardent, independent life pulsing through the bluest of blue veins – the inevitability of partial failure spurring him to attempt again and again the impossible magic of comprehending life in art.

With the transition indicated in the text of the novel by the first set of suspension points, the eye at the keyhole changes from the artist-observer's to the jailer's, and immediately the radical elusiveness of the prisoner becomes an infuriating taunt, an outrageous provocation to mayhem. For the artistic consciousness, the two essential activities are wonder and delight; for the totalitarian mentality, the one essential activity is control, manipulation – and therefore mysteries are intolerable, all souls must be "transparent" like the moving parts in a display-motor encased in clear plastic, so that they can at all times be completely accessible to control. Worse than opaque, Cincinnatus is seen here in defiant iridescence, continuing

to exercise the inner freedom that his jailers have long since re-
nounced because it was too dizzying, too difficult, interfered in too
many complicated ways with the simple, stupefying gratifications of
mutual manipulation. One can see why all "freaks," all who are
different, must be tortured in this world, and why it is an essential
quality of the perfected world of art *là-bas* to leave such creatures
wholly unmolested.

The peculiarly generalized nature of Cincinnatus as a character
serves the purpose of making him function in the novel as an embodiment of the generic possibilities of human freedom. Although
this is a novel about art, it is not, in the conventional sense, a literary
portrait of the artist because the artist here is conceived as an everyman, a paradigm of that life of consciousness which is common, at
least in potential, to all human beings. Cincinnatus in his cell deter-
mines to become a writer not because there is a streak of the aesthete
in him but because, finding himself a creature with consciousness in
an existence that offers nothing to explain that incredible fact, he
envisages art as the fullest, most human response to his own human
condition. In the passage we have been considering, Nabokov offers
us an external view of the mystery of individual life. Elsewhere, in
the pages quoted from Cincinnatus's journal, we get an eloquent
statement of that same mystery felt from within. The prisoner contemplates himself issuing from unknowable burning blackness, spinning like a top, headed he knows not where, and he wants desper-
ately to be able to capture in words that crazy, tormenting, somehow
stirring condition. "I have no desires, save the desire to express
myself – in defiance of all the world's muteness. How frightened I
am. How sick with fright. But no one shall take me away from
myself" (91). The perspective of *Invitation to a Beheading* is, I think,
finally political in Aristotle's sense of the term, not Machiavelli's. By
emphasizing an elaborately self-conscious art both as its medium and
its moral model, the novel affirms the tough persistence of humanity
in a world that is progressively more brutal and more subtle in its
attempts to take us away from ourselves.

NOTES

1. Simon Karlinsky, "Illusion, Reality, and Parody in Nabokov's Plays," *Wisconsin Studies in Contemporary Literature* 8.2 (1967): 268.

2. Vladimir Nabokov, *Invitation to a Beheading*, trans. Dimitri Nabokov in collaboration with the author (New York: G. P. Putnam's Sons, 1959), 12. Subsequent references in the text are to this edition.

3. Vladimir Nabokov, *The Gift*, trans. Michael Scammell with the collaboration of the author (New York: G. P. Putnam's Sons, 1963), 215.

4. Julian Moynahan, "A Russian Preface for Nabokov's *Beheading*," *Novel* 1.1 (1967): 16.

5. Vladimir Nabokov, *Nikolai Gogol* (New York: New Directions, 1961), 65.

Nabokov's *Invitation*: Literature as Execution

DALE PETERSON

*What draws the reader to the novel is the hope of warming his
shivering life with a death he reads about.*
—Walter Benjamin, "The Storyteller"

Anyone who has ever approached a Nabokov novel by way
of those peculiar literary vestibules known as "forewords" has had to
come to terms with a notoriously intimidating receptionist. Rarely
has an author gone to such trouble to discourage the sort of company he did not want his books to keep. Nabokov's prefaces and
interviews offer many examples of his abrasive integrity, but one
especially famous instance from a foreword of 1965 will suffice:
"*Despair*, in kinship with the rest of my books, has no social comment to make, no message to bring in its teeth. It does not uplift the
spiritual organ of man, nor does it show humanity the right exit."
Obviously, Vladimir Nabokov did not want to be liked for the wrong
reasons. He took great care to warn readers not to trespass on his
literary property if they were looking for relevant ideas or characters
to identify with. But the author's recommendation that we exclude
all but "aesthetic blisses" from our encounter with his prose has had
consequences that are not fortunate or fair; Nabokov's strong opinions have sometimes claimed more attention and respect than his far
more inviting texts.

Nabokov's prominent display of impatience with those who think
they can derive extraliterary pleasure and profit from literature has
reduced to protests or apologetics much criticism and commentary
on his work. Many reviews and some critical volumes have acclaimed
or condemned his compositions as pure, self-referential celebrations

of lexical play and imaginative artifice.[1] But Nabokov is more conscientious than playful in vehemently opposing the appropriation of his books to the service of "great ideas" or "real life." The militancy of his authorial voice on this subject suggests a degree of concern so intense as to involve a point of honor or even an ethic.

Although Nabokov enjoys a reputation as a serious artist, his work has never laid claim to the high seriousness of "moral fiction."[2] Even when he was at the height of his fame both as a Russian author and as an English one, his staunchest admirers have shied away from hailing the brilliant technical virtuoso as a notably large-hearted or large-minded genius. There has been, perhaps as a direct result of these reservations, a prolonged crisis over Nabokov's disappointing show as a humanitarian. Even those critics who most keenly appreciate an art that elaborates and then exposes human fabrications have yearned for the missing warmth of a tragic tone or at least the heartbeat of a humming humanism. Gleb Struve, for example, though enthusiastic about the sheer "combinational glee" behind Nabokov's creative power, cannot help regretting that Nabokov's characters, in the context of a passionately philanthropic Russian literature, "simply have no 'soul.'"[3] And Frank Kermode, even while proclaiming Nabokov a major novelist, fears that Anglo-American democrats will not take kindly to the Russian's narrative manner – "the personality that presides over his work is not amiable; we do not much care to be the objects of an author's contempt."[4] The nervousness expressed by these two appreciators of Nabokov indicates what can go wrong in general for readers who would like to be untroubled in their enjoyment of so evidently inventive a writer. The fact is that Nabokov's narratives refuse to promote the illusion that either characters or readers can be "cocreators" of the fate awaiting those enmeshed in a composition. With a consistency that seems perverse to some readers, Nabokov shatters not only the "realistic" illusion that characters determine their own destiny but also the modish illusion that readers can dictate the shape of an artistic construct. Surely Nabokov's habit of spoiling naive reading pleasures was deliberate. There is a principled intelligence at play in Nabokov's fictions – so much so that a close look should persuade us that Nabokov, appearances to the contrary, did write "moral fiction."

The sparse two hundred pages of *Invitation to a Beheading* offer an especially interesting example of the perceptual problem Nabokov's reader-trapping narratives create. At first glance, the work would seem to provide a textbook illustration of a twentieth-century "crystalline" fiction so memorably defined and deplored by Iris Murdoch in her influential article, "Against Dryness": "a small quasi-allegorical object portraying the human condition and not containing 'characters' in the 19th-century sense."[5] Murdoch's lucidly argued protest against self-conscious exercises in parable making is helpful; it labels the kind of experiment that *Invitation to a Beheading* appears to be and then attacks that kind of "modernist" fiction in the name of the truly humane values implicit in the richly representational novels of yesteryear. For now, this attack on a species of overtly fable-inventing fiction will serve nicely to introduce the understandable difficulty readers of traditional novels have with Nabokov's most autonomous, self-enclosed fictional world – the unnamed, unlocated, undated punitive mechanism that labors to execute the trapped, yet elusive, Cincinnatus C. Later, I show that what Iris Murdoch is for and against relates in unpredictable and amusingly complicated ways to the narrative art Nabokov practiced.

In Murdoch's argument, the trouble with the shapely, "crystalline" parables and fables that so cleverly refract an evident human condition is that they are, finally, too neat. A narrative form so overtly composed manifests a modern mind so abstracted and solipsistic that its main consolation is to play with symbolizations of experience. An honest literature, one adequate to lived twentieth-century reality, must be less, not more, form-conscious:

Our sense of form . . . can be a danger to our sense of reality. . . . Against the consolations of form, the clean crystalline work, the simplified fantasy-myth, we must pit the destructive power of the now so unfashionable naturalistic idea of character. Real people are destructive of myth, contingency is destructive of fantasy. (20)

Iris Murdoch wants to make room in narrative literature for life-like people to live and breathe. She is thinking fondly of those great Russian realists whose expansive narratives fully enact the play of personality and contingency that goes into the making of a destiny. For Murdoch, as for many other defenders of "novelistic" writing, there must be a return to a narrative manner that reproduces the fullness and complexity of the experienced world; the goal of a truly humanist literature, she writes, is to put us in a position to "rediscover a sense of the density of our lives."

Nabokov, too, as early as the 1930s, had seriously considered how literature might activate a respect for the true density of existence. It is a nice irony that his seemingly crystalline novel, *Invitation to a Beheading*, exposes, in the form of an opaque parable, why writing that purports to respect real life must not seek to reproduce it in verbal duplications. Viewed without prejudice, Nabokov's notoriously composed fictions exemplify an honest solution to the problem of perpetuating a humanist and ethical literature once we have seen through the conventions of nineteenth-century narrative realism.

Nabokov drafted the Russian original of *Invitation to a Beheading* in 1934, "in one fortnight of wonderful excitement and sustained inspiration"; the English translation of 1959 initiated the now famous series of "recastings" of Nabokov's Russian writings personally supervised by the author, and it displays the fewest traces of tampering and alteration of all his converted literary gems.[6] Yet, despite the fondness Nabokov publicly lavished on the Russian-born book he most esteemed, readers and critics have failed to reciprocate the author's strong pride in this particular literary brainchild. What has gone wrong, so far as I can judge, is that the daring quirkiness of the narrative has driven its distracted "explicators" to reduce the work to an intellectually manageable allegory of one sort or another.

If Nabokov's *Invitation* is, as Murdoch would have it, a "crystalline, quasi-allegorical" modernist work, it is a multifaceted and intellectually opaque creation, rather than a lucid reflection of a single reality. Most of the Russian émigré readers who first confronted the novel were sorely tempted to see Cincinnatus C.'s writhings and wrigglings inside a callously mismanaged detention center as Nabokov's disguised commentary on coping with totalitarianism in the twentieth century. But the logic of the book, when stripped down to a transparent political scenario, leads to conclusions that are maddening. It looks as if Nabokov, although himself a refugee from tyranny, can actually be irresponsible enough to advocate imaginative escapism as an adequate response to police states. If we read *Invitation* as political allegory, we have to invent a Nabokov who can make light of totalitarian threats by suggesting that acts of individual imaginative noncompliance and transcendence can dismantle them. Critics capable of inventing such a Nabokov have, understandably, never forgiven him his inhuman solipsism. "It is as if he has nothing to do with anything," observes one of these critics. "He nourishes himself; he attends to himself. He would sooner have visions than think, would sooner look into the specters he has created than what actually surrounds him."[7] Since the earliest reviews of his works, critics have assumed that Nabokov invites his readers to believe that imagination can rise above everything and anything, redeeming mundane hurts and losses. This is a claim careful readers will look into.

A few of Nabokov's Russian reviewers and many of his avid readers who know his work only in English look at *Invitation to a Beheading* as a camouflaged fable about the trials and tribulations of the artist in our insensitive, literal-minded mass societies. One brilliant article in particular, by the Russian poet Khodasevich, has, with strategic reprintings, virtually established the current orthodoxy that "the life of the artist and the life of a device in the consciousness of the artist" is Nabokov's basic, obsessive theme.[8] If there is to be a conventional wisdom about how to read Nabokov beyond the surface, it had better encourage readers to look for an artistic dilemma, not a social problem, behind the motley costuming of his extravagant fictions. But this approach, in effect, substitutes a more sophisticated style of allegorical reading for the more flat-footed, socially concerned interpretations we find in early critical attempts to take

Nabokov seriously. By 1959, in the first of his remarkably aggressive, reader-twitting forewords, Nabokov had learned how to frighten away relevance seekers who might try to treat him like "G. H. Orwell or other popular purveyors of illustrated ideas and publicistic fiction."[9] Ironically, Nabokov seems never to have suspected that his subtle art might suffer trivialization from a different quarter – from enthusiasts who would make an academic cult of all his works. There is a form of "vulgar aestheticism" that reduces Nabokov to the narrow profile of an artist whose every word is about artists attempting to make art or to make a place for art in the world. Only a badly impoverished understanding of Nabokov would read all his fictions as transparent celebrations of pattern-making minds whose "art" establishes a safe sanctuary for the free play of imagination. Fortunately, the actual dimensions of Nabokov's "crystalline" structures are broader. And if there is a trick to appreciating Nabokov's deep implications, it has to do with a willingness to stay attentive and honest to the plainly visible twists and turns that resist being simplified to the contours of straight allegory. Nowhere can we find a better example of Nabokov's deliberate intensification of "reading awareness" than in the puzzles that waylay us in *Invitation to a Beheading*.

The bold block letters that proclaim (in Russian as in English) Nabokov's startling book title also advertise something else – the complicity of anyone who has accepted an INVITATION TO A BEHEADING.[10] To hold the book open for reading is thus to expose oneself to being announced as a sensation seeker, an armchair executioner. Of course, not all readers will think to read their own conduct in this way. But they will try to enter into the promised action of this invitingly titled novel. And they will be confronted with a very strange spectacle, a seemingly alien set of juridical norms: "In accordance with the law the death sentence was announced to Cincinnatus C. in a whisper. All rose, exchanging smiles" (11) . How curious! What necessitates this concealment of a verdict that is a foreknown conclusion? The prisoner in the dock, as we learn from the framelike structure of chapter 1, has undergone a ritual sentence of condemnation; the defense counsel (required by law to be from the same womb as the prosecutor) has argued in precisely allotted words for "classic decapitation"; and the whispered legal formula delivered to Cincinnatus states that the execution occurs "with the gracious consent of the audience." What, then, is this charade of justice, this mock secrecy that consigns an improbably named victim (who vaguely evokes Roman virtue) to an improbably designed machinery of confinement (to a fairytale or operatic fortress) for the purpose of an arbitrary liquidation? The first paragraph is itself sufficient to induce a crisis of interpretation: What sort of world is this? Why have we been placed in it? Can anything "serious" be accomplished in, or taken from, such a fabulous world?

In the original Russian text, when we are literally at the turning point of the first page, we find one of the most extraordinary exposés of hidden literary pleasure in the whole self-conscious tradition of "modernist" writing:

> So we are nearing the end. The right-hand, still untasted part of the novel, which, during our delectable reading, we would lightly feel, mechanically testing whether there were still plenty left (and our fingers were always gladdened by the placid, faithful thickness) has suddenly, for no reason at all, become quite meager: a few minutes of quick reading, already downhill, and – O horrible!

The text catches us in a pretty tangle here. It makes public the secrets of our own entanglements with fiction, as if an eavesdropper had discovered us thrilling to the private knowledge that we can measure the vitality of persons and places by the flick of a thumb's thickness of pages and print. Yes, we do feel a certain power as we assist inevitability by thinning the fat right-hand text, slicing it away one razor-thin page at a time. Yet this elaborate situation is apparently raised to mind only as a metaphor for the sickening sensation that any victim of a vulgar tyranny might feel. Besides, this particular victim is not close to the end – or we are not – to judge by the remarkably full right-hand cluster of pages left to go. Still, this reassurance does not fully reassure. However prolonged the execution of Cincinnatus's fate seems from the perspective of page 2, however rich his symbolic identity promises to be, he is a character in a novel. That would seem inescapable.

Much of the rest of chapter 1, like the entire novel, explores the limits of an absurd confinement and the resources and recourses available to one who seems inescapably confined. Nabokov's exceptionally tricky narrative succeeds in making the seriousness of the confinement as problematic as the seriousness of the various escapes. Although what holds Cincinnatus imprisoned seems finally insubstantial and implausible and, although various escape routes seem accessible, Nabokov's sober design requires him to keep both Cincinnatus and us on the hooks of insoluble dilemmas. Within the first chapter alone, the structure that claims to hold Cincinnatus prisoner sometimes looks as sketchy as a rough draft by an incompetent novelist, sometimes as thick as a replica of a repressive bureaucratic regime. It is, of course, hard to tell the two structures apart; in each, characters are interchangeable and gross errors are erased from the record with no one held accountable. There is an analogy between a captive in the clutches of an autocratic power and a character in the meshes of a fictive plot, and Nabokov's writing makes us feel the terror of being subject to arbitrary revisions and reruns inside an announced plan of execution.

Cincinnatus C. offers us the spectacle of a prisoner or a character not yet dehumanized despite a verdict that offers him no choice but to collaborate in the obligatory steps toward his own extinction. That spectacle requires us to follow, chapter after chapter, a Chaplinesque pratfall comedy of endlessly attempted escapes and escapisms. The measure of Cincinnatus's humanness is in his indomitable, often ineffectual will to be elsewhere than in his ordained confinement. In no chapter is Cincinnatus, although imprisoned, fully "with it." Consider, from just the first chapter, the variety of his foiled departures: the waltz with the jailer beyond the cell in a "swoon's friendly embrace"; the "evening illumination" in which optical illusion transforms the posted prison rules, in fiery sunset, into a "reckless colorist's painting"; the extraordinary visit, on the wings of an imaginative parenthesis, to the romantic recesses of those "Tamara Gardens" where our prisoner met (and invented) the love of his life. Since Cincinnatus will succeed in making return flights to Tamara Gardens, it is worth hearing (in Russian) what sounds accompany his transport there: "Tam . . . Tam . . . Zelyónoye, muravchátoye Tam, támoshniye kholmý, tamléniye prudóv, tamtatám dalyókovo orkéstra." 'There . . . There . . . The green, turfy There, thence its local hills, the languid thrumming of its ponds, the tum-ta-tum of a distant band'.[11] Even the translation of this passage shows that Cincinnatus has soared into the realm of faerie. But when one considers that the Russian *tam* is the poetic equivalent of the French *là*, it is clear that the prisoner's unaided imaginative ecstasy has carried him to the borders of that Baudelairean "beyond" whence come all emanations of bliss and perfection.[12] Even on the first day of his confinement, Cincinnatus C. has learned to exercise that fragile human release of being more "there" than "here."

For all the multiple imaginative avenues that seem to conduct Cincinnatus "out of it," each chapter rings to a close with a more or less effective restoration of the humiliating and absurd confinement. The difficulty of achieving genuine escape is compounded in the Russian text by the cruel pun on the term *zaklyuchenie*, which all-inclusively evokes a "lock up" in the sense of both a "confinement" and a "conclusion." Wherever Cincinnatus turns, however he turns, an authority's (or an author's) foregone conclusion encompasses him. Yet there is one other "out," one other defense left to the prisoner:

> On the table glistened a clean sheet of paper and, distinctly outlined against this whiteness, lay a beautifully sharpened pencil, as long as the life of any man except Cincinnatus. . . . An enlightened descendant of the index finger. Cincinnatus wrote: "In spite of everything, I am comparatively. . . . " (12)

The prisoner is granted the fetching opportunity of transcribing his identity. The privilege of writing offers any prisoner, any character, the chance to translate his existence into another dimension, and this would seem a marvelous emancipation indeed. Yet this instrument of escape has a double edge. Nabokov's language playfully recognizes the latent executive powers of the as yet unwielded pencil – in Russian, it is the promising regal extension of the "pointing" or "dictating" finger (*ukazatel'nyi perst'*). But who or what commands those powers of execution? Why is every man's life (except Cincinnatus's) as long as the offered pencil? Who controls the public articulations of prisoners and characters? We readers are invited to think on such subjects.

If we give serious contemplation to the plot that encompasses Cincinnatus, we can appreciate the complexity of Nabokov's crystalline parable. The closer we look at Cincinnatus's entrapment, the better we can see that it is simultaneously political, philosophical, marital – and, of course, ineluctably fictional. Nabokov's captive has been apprehended and condemned for the sin of "gnostical turpitude" – he will be executed "with the gracious consent of the audience" although, as he is fully aware, he has been "fashioned so painstakingly." Cincinnatus's fatal offense is that he is opaque; unlike the better-suited residents of the "habitus" he finds himself in, he cannot be seen through at first glance, he cannot be understood at the first word. He is, unforgivably, a character who is hard to read. The society that incarcerates Cincinnatus has shown its true colors to him in a dusty little museum on Second Boulevard:

> [T]here was a collection of rare, marvelous objects, but all the townsmen except Cincinnatus found them just as limited and transparent as they did each other. *That which does not have a name does not exist.* Unfortunately everything had a name. (26)

Cincinnatus is trapped by a society that only respects and responds to what is labeled; he is romantically attached to a wife who extends her favors to any named need – "Little Marthe did it again today. . . . it's such a small thing, and it's such a relief to a man" (31). The name of his public defender, the one who advocates a clear-cut "classic decapitation," is Roman Vissarionovich – a sly allusion (Novel, the son of Vissarion) to Vissarion Belinsky, the first critic-propagandist for a social-minded realism in Russian literature. Cincinnatus seems designed to serve as the perfect fall guy for a tyranny of vulgar practicality.

But there are weaknesses in the structure that holds Cincinnatus captive. Well before the prisoner suspects that he resides in a "hastily assembled and painted world," we are puzzling over the propped-up domain that contains and surrounds Cincinnatus. The scenes in the courtroom and in the jail are transparently made up of makeup and stage sets; the judge's mouth looks as though it has to be unglued from the prisoner's ear, and we later look on as the ungluing of a red beard and a leather apron transforms Rodion, the jailer, into Rodrig, the prison director. We notice that both of these "Rods" move with suspicious stiffness, literally accompanied by creaking joints and squeaking backs. Besides the telltale traces of costuming and special effects that weaken the solidity of this imprisoning world, Cincinnatus also observes that his society is in a state of entropic decline. An age of gravity-defying levitation and aspiration has passed; airplanes and even automobiles can only be glimpsed in sideshows or back copies of glossy magazines. Clearly, past accomplishments dwarf present realities. Cincinnatus is held in thralldom by the mental and technological equivalent of Toyland, by a company of strutting players leaping aboard little electric "wagonets" or spring-powered two-seat "clocklets." Finally, it would seem that this pathetically patched, outmoded society cannot finish off its prisoners properly without their genial collaboration. No execution is complete without a ritual embrace, a public collusion between victim and "fate-mate." Gradually Cincinnatus and the reader alike come to understand that the beheading has been postponed so that the performer of the execution, M'sieur Pierre, can play at being a fellow prisoner who empathizes with the condemned victim. But this charade of amity is so flawed that a proper execution continues to be delayed. Given the obvious fraud and naiveté that mar the effectiveness of the confining society, what keeps Cincinnatus so long enthralled?

The imagination of Cincinnatus C., despite its better intimations, remains attached to a conceivably improved version of the given world. Like so many earlier and later Nabokov amphibians, half in and half out of mundane reality, Cincinnatus suffers the torment and dislocation of an agnostic Gnostic. He cannot quite bring himself to shake off the blandishments of tangible pleasures, even though his own intellectual conclusions restrict reliable joys to an uncarnal, disembodied realm. The prisoner's entrapment, against his own better judgment, is announced in his first interview with the defense counsel:

> I am surrounded by some sort of wretched specters. . . . They torment me as can torment only senseless visions, bad dreams, dregs of delirium, the drivel of nightmares and everything that passes down here for real life. In theory one would wish to wake up. But wake up I cannot without outside help. (36)

Imprisoned in a claptrap world and yearning, naturally enough, for a "physically feasible freedom," Cincinnatus's gifted imagination plays tricks on him:

> [I]nstantly he imagined, with such sensuous clarity as though it all was a fluctuating corona emanating from him, the town beyond the shallowed river, the town, from every point of which one could see – now in this vista, now in that, now in crayon, and now in ink – the tall fortress within which he was. . . . in the confining phenomena of life his reason sought out a possible trail, some kind of vision danced before his eyes. . . . and, even though in reality everything in this city was always quite dead and awful by comparison with the secret life of Cincinnatus and his guilty flame, even though he knew this perfectly well and knew also that there was no hope, yet at this moment he still longed to be on those bright familiar streets. (73–75)

Goaded on by his futile, foredoomed hope for a literal escape within the confines of the here and now, this prisoner, this character, falls for all the cheap literary and vicarious resolutions by which the imagination tries to buy time or achieve release:

> Involuntarily yielding to the temptation of logical development, involuntarily (be careful, Cincinnatus!) forging into a chain all the things that were quite harmless as long as they remained unlinked, he inspired the meaningless with meaning, and the lifeless with life. (155)

In this behavior, be it noted, Cincinnatus strongly resembles the unwary reader of serious books. The paths of intellect and the streets the imagination stalks are just as vivid as any given path or street, but they do exist in a different dimension altogether.

It should come as no surprise that Cincinnatus comes closest to escaping his vulgar fate and the "banal senseless dreams of escape" it encourages when he accepts the seemingly useless diversion of writing. Writing becomes the occasion for Cincinnatus to transport his consciousness into communion with that other self that freely wanders in a realm of pure potentiality. Through writing, Cincinnatus can both claim and grant himself an irrevocable furlough from his involuntary servitude to the tyranny of the evident: "[P]art of my thoughts is always crowding around the invisible umbilical cord that joins this world to something" (53). Writing, in its expression of an intelligence free of the burden of immediate time and space, promises to become an actual vehicle of emancipation large enough to transport all us characters and prisoners there (*tam, là*) where supple form is given to all the patterns it has been our pleasure vaguely to preconceive. In practice, though, writing is, for Cincinnatus, a "criminal exercise" in an ironic way: it is as much a reminder of his prison bars as it is a ticket to liberation. Cincinnatus cannot invest full confidence in writing as his surest exit from entrapment; he never knows whether he will have time or talent enough to combine commonplace words into whole lines of "live iridescence." Worse yet, his nontransparent, opaque prose has literally no place in his given society, and it is hard to write without "at least the theoretical possibility of having a reader." But the worst failure of self-expression as a way out of confinement finally becomes apparent in one of the prisoner's last jottings:

> My words all mill about in one spot. . . . Envious of poets. How wonderful it must be to speed along a page and, right from the page, where only a shadow continues to run, to take off into the blue. The untidiness, sloppiness of an execution, of all the manipulations, before and after. How cold the blade, how smooth the ax's grip. With emery paper. I suppose the pain of parting will be red and loud. The thought, when written down, becomes less oppressive, but some thoughts are like a cancerous tumor: you express it, you excise it, and it grows back worse than before. (194)

This admission is sinister in at least two ways. It announces the inescapable truth that although writing may freely objectify any conception, it always responds to the dictates of a consciousness dominated by its own felt compulsions. The passage also suggests the lethal finality of all successful executions, physical and poetic, corporal and verbal.

Nabokov sees to it that Cincinnatus's writing expresses a painful vacillation between departures "there" and returns "here." The poetic rhythms that transport Cincinnatus's being into residence in the "unreal estate" of *tam* and Tamara Gardens are continually interrupted by a different, rougher music, the countersound of *tūt* (with *ū* pronounced "oo," as in t*oo*t), the here and now: "Tūpóyeh tūt, podpyórtoyeh i zápertoyeh chetóyū 'tvyérduh,' tyómnaya tyūr'má, v kotórūyū zaklyūchyón neūyómnuh voyūshchee ūzhas." 'The dense "dead-end," propped up and locked up by its pair of *d*'s, a dark dungeon in which an unconstrainedly howling horror is confined'.[13] Cincinnatus's ability to waver between here and there teases the reader unmercifully. Yet it is profoundly right that we should be hard pressed to place this character. Had we but known, we could have found the novel's maddening, tricky conclusion foreshadowed in Cincinnatus's first long self-communing passage:

[O]ur vaunted waking life . . . is semi-sleep, an evil drowsiness into which penetrate in grotesque disguise the sounds and sights of the real world, flowing beyond the periphery of the mind – as when you hear during sleep a dreadful insidious tale because a branch is scraping on the pane. . . .

But how I fear awakening! How I fear that second, or rather split second, already cut short then, when, with a lumberjack's grunt – But what is there to fear? Will it not be for me simply the shadow of an ax, and shall I not hear the downward vigorous grunt with the ear of a different world? Still I am afraid! One cannot write it off so easily. (92)

Perhaps a poetic sensibility can translate all experiencc into a different dimension of extended, purer meanings. But, as the writer's treacherous pun suggests, to write off given details as metaphors for something else might only be possible inside texts.

Even as Cincinnatus struggles to express his extradimensional being, Nabokov has him note: "I am trembling over the paper, chewing the pencil through to the lead, hunching over to conceal myself from the door through which a piercing eye stings me in the nape" (91). The reference is, of course, to the unremitting peephole observation that is one of the basic terms of the prisoner's confinement. But only the most literal-minded readers will imagine that the only pair of eyes peering in are those of the red-bearded Rodion, personifying Red Russian totalitarianism. And even such readers, one would hope, would have to see more after the thought-jarring narrative interruption Nabokov hurls into the eleventh chapter:

The subject will now be the precious quality of Cincinnatus; his fleshy incompleteness; the fact that the greater part of him was in a quite different place, while only an insignificant portion of it was wandering, perplexed, here. . . . Cincinnatus's face . . . with gliding eyes, eerie eyes of changeable shade, was, in regard to its expression, something absolutely inadmissible by the standards of his surroundings. . . . the light outline of his lips, seemingly not quite fully drawn but touched by a master of masters . . . the fluttering movements of his empty, not-yet-shaded-in hands. . . . all of this, analyzed and studied, still could not fully explain Cincinnatus. . . . and all this so teased the observer as to make him long to tear apart, cut to shreds, destroy utterly this brazen elusive flesh, and all that it implied and expressed, all that impossible, dazzling freedom – enough, enough – do not walk anymore, Cincinnatus, lie down on your cot, so you will not arouse, will not irritate. (120–22)

Surely the long-frustrated, much-teased lover of "realistic" character at last recognizes his own eyes, blazing with ire, reflected in this cleverly rendered peek at Cincinnatus's enraged and nameless "observer"? After all, neither prisoners nor "realistic" characters are rightly entitled to the privacy that could protect them from a penetrating understanding of their motivations and behavior. They should be transparent examples to us all.

There is, to put it mildly, a remarkable coincidence between the implications of the passage just quoted and the brilliant thesis expounded in a few paragraphs in Walter Benjamin's essay of 1936 on the Russian storyteller Nikolai Leskov:

In this solitude of his, the reader of a novel seizes upon his material more jealously than anyone else. He is ready to make it completely his own, to devour it, as it were. Indeed, he destroys, he swallows up the material as the fire devours logs in the fireplace. . . . The nature of the character in a novel . . . says that the "meaning" of his life is revealed only in his death. . . . The reader of a novel actually does look for human beings from whom he derives the "meaning of life." Therefore he must, no matter what, know in advance that he will share their experience of death: if need be their figurative death – the end of the novel – but preferably their actual one. How do the characters make him understand that death is already waiting for them? . . . That is the question which feeds the reader's consuming interest in the events of the novel.[14]

For Benjamin, the reader of the nineteenth-century novel, or "book of life," has quite literally become a consumer who feeds on the vitality offered by sacrificed characters; for Nabokov, the observer of character is always in essence a predator who needs to expose the vital parts of a maddeningly elusive, opaque prey. Both the reading of novels and the analysis of character are acts of cannibalism at a metaphoric level; the ultimate aim of the activity is to suck the final marrow of meaning from the perfectly exposed innards of a perfectly executed figure.

The prisoner Cincinnatus, with Nabokov's full complicity, comes to understand the lethal design behind the arbitrary confinement he suffers. He and we are given the chance to see viciousness and buffoonery combined in the valedictory speech delivered by pudgy, chummy M'sieur Pierre, the plot's hatchet man:

> Kind gentlemen . . . first of all and before anything else, allow me to outline by means of a few deft strokes [!] what has already been accomplished by me.
>
> . . . You gentlemen are of course aware of the reasons for the amusing mystification that is required by the tradition of our craft. After all, how would it be if I had announced myself right at the start and offered my friendship to Cincinnatus C.? This, gentlemen, would have certainly resulted in repelling him, frightening him, antagonizing him – in short, I would have committed a fatal blunder.
>
> . . . I need not explain how precious to the success of our common undertaking [!] is that atmosphere of warm camaraderie which, with the help of patience and kindness, is gradually created between the sentenced and the executor of the sentence. . . .
>
> . . . Sometimes, in peaceful silence, we would sit side by side, almost with our arms about each other, each thinking his own twilight thoughts, and the thoughts of both of us would flow together like rivers when we opened our lips to speak. . . . The results are before you. We grew to love each other, and the structure of Cincinnatus's soul is as well known to me as the structure

of his neck. Thus it will be not an unfamiliar, terrible somebody but a tender friend that will help him mount the crimson steps, and he will surrender himself to me without fear – forever, for all death. Let the will of the public be carried out! (172–73, 175)

This speech uncovers the subhuman vulgarity of the scheme of execution that has been clamped around Cincinnatus. Through it, Nabokov perpetrates a monstrous, double-headed parody. The executioner's pretense of all-knowing intimacy is peculiar to totalitarian regimes – and to the authors of realistic novels.[15] However one looks at Cincinnatus – as political prisoner, unawakened Gnostic, or fictional character – he seems inextricably trapped, even though what victimizes him is a grossly inept and transparently fraudulent tyranny of appearances. The ultimate drama of Nabokov's book is Cincinnatus's struggle to stay the promised end and, through his foreknowledge of the fraudulent omniscience of the confining system, thwart the will to execute a design in which he is tempted to believe. Can a novelist, even one as ingenious as Nabokov, liberate characters from the cannibalism of consumers and free prisoners from the designs of tyrants?

We are nearing the novel's controversial ending. Before the author springs it on us, the prisoner becomes better schooled and skilled in certain "criminal exercises" that obliterate the bars and stripes of confining appearances. When the very thick of the Tamara Gardens stands revealed as a fool's paradise concocted by a tourist-trapping city management, Cincinnatus discovers that his endlessly regenerative imagination cannot be divested of its original shares of bliss: "[E]xploring the surroundings with a diligent eye, he easily removed the murky film of night from the familiar lawns and also erased from them the superfluous lunar dusting, so as to make them exactly as they were in his memory" (187). Even when we can see the perfect forms of elsewhere as optical rearrangements of the here and now, they need not lose their permanent imaginative validity. A little later, a strategically timed bit of escape artistry by nature's own Houdini, an elusive, erratic moth, also strengthens the prisoner's confidence in successful flight. This glorious moth is – by no accident – the most alive character in the book; described with Nabokov's unerring eye for naturalistic detail, its majestic visionary wings with their "perpetually open eyes" elude entrapment by the snares of this world – "But to me your daytime is dark, why did you disturb my slumber?" (204). It is immediately after the moth evades the jailer that Cincinnatus formulates his own worst failure and best hope. He has fallen into "the dead end of this life" (*tūpik tūtoshnei zhizni*) by letting the specious logic of daylight realism close in on him: "I should not have sought salvation within its confines. . . . [I was] like a man grieving because he has recently lost in his dreams some thing that he never had had in reality, or hoping that tomorrow he would dream that he found it again" (205). What Cincinnatus should have realized from the first days of his confinement or conclusion was that he was a captive of his own trust in semblances and verisimilitude. Like all Nabokov's exiled dreamers, he is a "prisoner of Zembla."

It finally happens, inescapably, that we turn the last page. Our leading character is on the block finally about to be executed, as promised, to have his unacceptable opaqueness ended. Here is what occurs:

[O]ne Cincinnatus was counting, but the other Cincinnatus had already stopped heeding the sound of the unnecessary count which was fading away in the distance; and, with a clarity he had never experienced before – at first almost painful, so suddenly did it come, but then suffusing him with joy, he reflected: why am I here? Why am I lying like this? And, having asked himself these simple questions, he answered them by getting up and looking around.

. . . Everything was coming apart. Everything was falling. A spinning wind was picking up and whirling: dust, rags, chips of painted wood, bits of gilded plaster, pasteboard bricks, posters; an arid gloom fleeted; and amidst the dust, and the falling things, and the flapping scenery, Cincinnatus made his way in that direction where, to judge by the voices, stood beings akin to him. (222–23)

What has happened here? Has a character been executed? Are we to believe that this character has escaped execution?

Some will protest this trick ending and will condemn the author for trying to get away with double-talk. Some will decide for themselves what really has happened and will resolve any confusion by reaching their own conclusions. Perhaps some dyed-in-the-wool "modernists" will appreciate the trickery for trickery's sake. But what we all have to cope with, for as long as we face it, is the absolutely unhidden duplicity of this novel's ending. Two Cincinnatuses are present at the novel's close, and it is clearly possible to see either as dominant. In one reading, the basic Cincinnatus is the mortal, "existential" one (the one who counts); like Tolstoy's Ivan Ilyich he achieves a sudden, painful, joyous clarity as the axe falls, leaving us the burden of his posthumous, unlived wisdom. In another view, the basic Cincinnatus is the deathless "metaphysical" one, whose punning, dualistic consciousness ("why am I here? Why am I lying like this?") awakens itself from a needless collusion with vulgar appearances.[16] The novelist is obviously letting us have it both ways, even as he pulls down the props of a fiction that has so well housed such ambiguous significance. The novelist blatantly refuses to assume responsibility for providing a credible, conclusive ending. Quite understandably, this deliberately staged lack of finish makes us nervous.

Last words, whether or not they become famous, receive the attention true conclusions deserve, and not even Nabokov's artful dodging can forestall the tendency to draw conclusions from endings. So, when Cincinnatus leaves the staging that was to execute him and makes his final turn toward an offstage dimension where kindred beings seem to lurk, it is natural to feel the author's full force pushing open an escape clause. In the Russian, those murky beings toward whom Cincinnatus makes his way are literally his "similars," perhaps the equivalent of Baudelaire's *semblables*, and thus hypocriti-

cal readers. Cincinnatus seems about to join whatever posterity literary characters enjoy or, possibly, to blend into the company of us
readers, his Baudelairean brethren in the crime of opaqueness. In
any case, Nabokov startles us into thinking about a direction in
which characters and victims can achieve liberation. Nabokov char-
acteristically springs his variously trapped characters loose at the end
of his novels.[17] He invites us readers to executions that he then
shows to be literary frauds; he is not a writer who wants us to believe
that characters can have their heads entirely or lose them cleanly.
Literary characters, like the hopelessly imprisoned victims of any
tyranny, cannot escape crude, inhuman execution unless they can
survive in a richly imagined afterlife beyond the text's last word.
Human vitality is opaque; it shimmers with the aura of a multivari-
able dimensionality that is impossible to catch in the commonplace
mirrors of daylight realism. Thus we return by a long route to the
argument that started this discussion: What shape should "moral
fiction" take?

———

Among its many virtues, Nabokov's *Invitation* remains valuable as
a crystalline parable in defense of modernist narrative; insofar as
Cincinnatus is the victim of a conspiracy to penetrate his privacy and
reduce him to a "realized" character, his story is an ethical counter-
statement to the mode and manners of conventional literary realism.
By a curious twist, Nabokov's Cincinnatus exists to endorse the same
standard Iris Murdoch advocates in her manifesto for a return to
narratives that reproduce the density of people and events: "Our
current picture of freedom encourages a dream-like facility; whereas
what we require is a renewed sense of the difficulty and complexity
of the moral life and the opacity of persons" (20). Literature ought to
foster an alertness to, and even a reverence for, the messiness and
mystery of real existence – on that proposition Murdoch and
Nabokov can agree. But *how* literary form fosters a respect for life's
complication was a matter of great and consistent ethical interest to

Nabokov; he cared enough to declare conscientious objection to all forms of the illusion that serious art could duplicate reality.

Some may find it convenient to believe that rampant exhibitionism motivates those writers who remind us that their characters and events are actually lively words in sequence.[18] For Nabokov, however, such reminders of literature's patterned simulation of experience are essential to decent relations with one's reader. The issue is a matter of philosophical integrity and professional ethics; moral fiction is fiction that makes no pretense of being identical with given reality, or even a substitute for it. With his extraordinary gift for minute observation and remembering, Nabokov could have been a master illusionist of literary realism. But his choice was always to spoil the illusion of lifelike narrative so that the reader would become conscious of the true chasm between lived experience and imaginative activity.

In "Pushkin, or Verity and Verisimilitude," an important untranslated article that appeared in a Parisian literary journal just before the publication of *Invitation to a Beheading*, Nabokov confirmed the moral seriousness implicit in his self-imposed fictiveness:

> Is it possible to imagine in its full reality the life of another, to relive it oneself and transfer it intact onto paper? I doubt it; in fact, it makes one tempted to believe that thought itself, in fixing its beam on the life history of a person, inevitably deforms it. Thus, it can only be the verisimilar, and not the veritable truth, that the mind perceives. . . . And yet what rapture for a daydreaming Russian to depart into Pushkin's world! These visions are probably fraudulent and the real Pushkin would not recognize himself in them, but if I invest in them a bit of that same love I experience in reading his poems, won't what I make of this imaginary life be something resembling the poet's works, if not himself? . . . Thus one would like to think that what we call art is, in essence, truth's picture window; one has to know how to frame it, that's all.[19]

This statement proclaims a mature sense of the necessary relations between factuality, art, and conscience. Actual experience is inimitable and evanescent. Even accounts of one's own experience are always facsimiles of permanently lost vital facts. We can only put our bliss into safekeeping or retard the moment-by-moment extinction of our personal and cultural estate by creating consciously aesthetic corollaries to the losses we mourn and dimly recall. The only permanence we perceive is artificial; the only character we possess we have ourselves fashioned; and the only responsible art is a moral fiction that lets us know we are contemplating a stand-in, a parody version, of an opaque actuality that can never be articulated conclusively. It is because Cincinnatus C. is so very sketchy and so very metaphorical that he can retain some semblance of our true humanity within the execution chamber of literature. It is true to Nabokov's ethical form to employ a coup de grâce to assert that the character most read about and read into has an unpredictable vitality that eludes the narrative's reach. In the end, Nabokov helps his characters leap into a different dimension of existence; there is, after all, a posttextual life that authors can do nothing about.

The epigraph to *Invitation to a Beheading* is a riddle worth contemplating:

> Comme un fou se croit Dieu
> nous nous croyons mortels
> Delalande, *Discours sur les ombres*

Trying to unpack all that wit into English is a challenge, but it might unravel as a passage from *A Discourse on Shades*, by "A. Farland," to the effect that we believe we are mortal just as a madman believes he is God. Delalande, Nabokov's "favorite writer," is himself an invented, apparently Gnostic sage, and the shades he discusses bring to mind *hombres* as much as Platonic images of supernal forms. Whatever the facts of the case (and they are all shadowy), the wisdom hinted at the beginning of Nabokov's great experimental novel whispers the radical, subversive, antirealistic news that we all inhabit, ultimately, a world constructed of similes and syllogisms, analogies and metaphors. The word from A. Farland to the wise among us recommends that we have the humility and the hard sense to recognize that the real world always escapes us. The extended parable Nabokov introduces with that wisdom encourages a breakthrough beyond the confines of an absurd and humorless "realism" that accepts likely facsimiles for actual truths. The novelist has designed the visible duplicity of *Invitation to a Beheading* to liberate present and future victims from the drab prison houses of authoritarian language. Here again, as in so much else, the wit and wisdom of Nabokov resemble (in an unforeseen coincidence he would have relished) the good-humored, philosophically sophisticated modernism of Wallace Stevens:

From time immemorial the philosophers and other sane painters have daubed the sky with dazzle paint. But it all comes down to the proverbial six feet of earth in the end. . . . Why not fill the sky with scaffolds and stairs, and go about like genuine realists?[20]

NOTES

1. The titles of several book-length studies point to the trend pursued by many of Nabokov's loyal defenders; see, for instance, Page Stegner's *Escape into Aesthetics* (New York: Morrow, 1966) or Julia Bader's *Crystal Land: Artifice in Nabokov's English Novels* (Berkeley: University of California Press, 1972). In Tony Tanner's *City of Words: American Fiction 1950–1970* (London: Jonathan Cape, 1971), an influential chapter entitled "On Lexical Playfields" goes so far as to promote the heroic aesthetic self-liberations achieved in the fictive games of Nabokov and Borges. It is precisely this coldly intellectual play of devices and artifices that has elicited the strongest negative criticism; see, especially, William H. Gass's "Mirror, Mirror" in *Fiction and the Figures of Life* (New York: Vintage-Knopf, 1972).

2. The phrase has again been placed in critical currency by John Gardner's remarkably intemperate tract against "aesthetic game-players," *On Moral Fiction* (New York: Basic Books, 1978). Fortunately, there have been of late some exceptionally well-argued philosophical and ethical appreciations of Nabokov's visible artifices; I think especially of Elizabeth W. Bruss's chap-

ter on Nabokov in her *Autobiographical Acts* (Baltimore: The Johns Hopkins University Press, 1976) 127–62; and Ellen Pifer, "On Human Freedom and Inhuman Art: Nabokov," in *Slavic and East European Journal* 22 (1978): 52–63. Also, Dabney Stuart's *Nabokov: The Dimensions of Parody* (Baton Rouge: Louisiana State University Press, 1978) rightly emphasizes the serious playfulness that explodes with ridicule certain received modes of literary perception.

3. Gleb Struve, *Russkaia literatura v izgnanii* (New York: Chekhov Publishing House, 1956), 285–87. To be exact, Struve's comment refers to the characters of Nabokov's appropriate nom de plume, Sirin, the name of a mythical, magical bird.

4. Frank Kermode, "Aesthetic Bliss," *Encounter* (June 1960): 81–86.

5. Iris Murdoch, "Against Dryness: A Polemical Sketch," *Encounter* (January 1961): 16–20.

6. On the book's gestation, see Alfred Appel, Jr., "An Interview with Vladimir Nabokov," in *Wisconsin Studies in Contemporary Literature* 8 (1967): 127–52; for an analysis of its metamorphosis into English, see Jane Grayson, *Nabokov Translated* (New York: Oxford, 1977), 119–24.

7. Georgii Adamovich, *Odinochestvo i svoboda* (New York: Chekhov Publishing House, 1955), 217. (All translations are mine.)

8. Khodasevich's essay of 1937, "On Sirin," was translated in *TriQuarterly* 17 (1970): 96–101; before then, R.H.W. Dillard's influential "Not Text, but Texture: The Novels of Vladimir Nabokov," in *The Hollins Critic* 3 (1966): 1–12, had established the expectation that Nabokov wrote about artist figures. Despite this trend, the same issue of *TriQuarterly* contains Robert Alter's pioneering, multileveled discussion of political and artistic fable making in *"Invitation to a Beheading*: Nabokov and the Art of Politics," 41–59 (reprinted in the present volume).

9. Vladimir Nabokov, Foreword, *Invitation to a Beheading* (New York: Capricorn, 1965), 6. Hereafter references to this work will be cited parenthetically within the text from this edition.

10. Literally, in Russian, *Invitation to an Execution*; the novel was first published as *Priglashenie na kazn'* (Paris: Dom Knigi, 1938).

11. *Priglashenie* 14. Like Nabokov, I have allowed myself a deliberately loose auditory transcription and free translation, the better to convey the extraordinary word weaving that blends sonorities and semantic units into new chains of association.

12. The reference is, of course, to Baudelaire's "L'Invitation au voyage" (1855), which calls for a dream transport back "there" to a once glimpsed world of invulnerable harmonies – "Là, tout n'est qu'ordre et beauté, / Luxe, calme et volupté" (There, naught but grace and measure, / Luxuriance, calm and pleasure). Alter confirms this association (45).

13. *Priglashenie* 83. The Russian makes an ingenious auditory pun on *tūt* ("ici") and on the Old Slavonic name for the letter *t*, which also means, in modern Russian, "firmly"; the howling horror is the *ū* sound held in by the firm *t*s. In an early review in the Parisian Russian journal *Sovremennye zapiski* 68 (1939): 474–77, P. Bitsilli discusses the device of the pun as a mode of "rehabilitating" hidden dimensions of meaning covered over by dull dictionary definitions of reality. See D. Barton Johnson's translation and commentary in *A Book of Things about Nabokov*, ed. Carl R. Proffer (Ann Arbor, Mich.: Ardis, 1974), 65–69, hereafter cited as *Book of Things*.

14. Walter Benjamin, "The Storyteller: Reflections on the Work of Nikolai Leskov," in *Illuminations* (New York: Schocken, 1969), 100–101.

15. *Invitation* includes a parody of encyclopedic "realism" in the form of *Quercus*, a thousand-page biography of an oak and the history it has seen; Cincinnatus borrows it from the prison library and notes, "It seemed as though the author were sitting with his camera somewhere among the topmost branches of the Quercus, spying out and catching his prey" (123).

16. By this reading, *Invitation* is what Mircea Eliade would define as a classic example of Gnostic literature:

[These texts] stress, on the one hand, the soul's fall into Matter (Life) and the mortal "sleep" that ensues, and, on the other hand, the soul's extraterrestrial origin. . . . Since they are Spiritual Beings of extraterrestrial origin, the Gnostics do not admit that their home is "here," in this world. . . . Once waked from his mortal sleep, the Gnostic understands that . . . he has no *real* relation with Life, the World, and History. . . . The sufferings that constitute every human life vanish at the moment of waking. Waking, which is at the same time an *anamnesis*, finds expression in an indifference to History.

See Eliade's *Myth and Reality* (New York: Harper, 1963), 132–34. For a reading of Cincinnatus as a Gnostic hero-buffoon who will not collaborate with a vulgar orthodoxy, see Julian Moynahan, "A Russian Preface for Nabokov's *Beheading*," *Novel* 1 (1967): 12–18.

17. The visible servitude of so many Nabokov characters is, as William Carroll rightly argues, a transparent reminder that they are intermediaries at the mercy of the author's and the reader's need to compose a finite end: "Nabokov's characters are 'galley slaves' in that they know themselves subject to inhuman and autocratic powers; and we (and a few of them) know that the 'galley' is both man's physical situation and the printer's proof taken from composed type" ("Nabokov's Signs and Symbols," in *Book of Things*, 203–17).

18. See Gardner: "To people who care about events and ideas . . . linguistic opacity suggests indifference to the needs and wishes of the reader and to whatever ideas might be buried under all that brush. And since one reason we read fiction is our hope that we will be moved by it, finding characters we can enjoy and sympathize with, an academic striving for opacity suggests, if not misanthropy, a perversity or shallowness" (69).

19. Vladimir Nabokoff-Sirine, "Pouchkine ou le vrai et le vraisemblable," *Nouvelle revue française* 48 (1937): 362–78. My translation is of excerpts from pages 367, 369, and 377.

20. Wallace Stevens, Letter to William Stanley Braithwaite, 5 December 1921, *Letters of Wallace Stevens*, ed. Holly Stevens (New York: Knopf, 1972), 223.

The Otherworld in *Invitation to a Beheading*

VLADIMIR E. ALEXANDROV

Attention to the central role of metaphysics in Nabokov's writings is a relatively recent development, one that follows decades of primary scholarly focus on the metaliterariness of his art. Under this new form of scrutiny, Nabokov's novels, stories, poems, and discursive works emerge as embodying a sui generis faith in a transcendent, timeless, and beneficent realm that appears to affect everything in the material world and to provide for personal immortality. Nabokov's designation for this dimension of being was "the otherworld," and a cardinal tenet of his faith was that one can have only intuitions about it; no certainty is possible.[1]

Invitation to a Beheading (*Priglashenie na kazn'*) camouflages its otherworldly concerns less than any of Nabokov's other Russian novels. Its allegorical surface is the story of the final weeks and execution of a prisoner in a banal future tyranny. But unlike such familiar dystopias as Evgenii Zamiatin's *We*, Aldous Huxley's *Brave New World*, and George Orwell's *1984*, which are concerned primarily with questions of political and social organization and with their psychological and ethical implications, Nabokov's novel focuses on the protagonist's relation to a metaphysical reality.[2] Indeed, as Julian Moynahan has suggested, and as Sergej Davydov has demonstrated in detail, much in the life of Cincinnatus C. is modeled on major Gnostic topoi.[3] Nabokov in effect hinted at this himself when he changed the definition of Cincinnatus's crime from the general "gnoseologicheskaia gnusnost'" ("gnoseological turpitude") in the original Russian to the much more specific "gnostical turpitude" in the English translation (72/80). The appearance of Gnostic motifs in many of his works suggests that he must have found some aspects of this ancient worldview congruent with his own.

It may have been the dominance of metaphysical issues in *Invitation to a Beheading* – and their extension into aesthetics and ethics – that led Nabokov, in his preface to the English translation of the novel, to dismiss the possibility that the Bolshevik and Nazi regimes served as prototypes for it or that Kafka influenced it (5–6). In marked contrast to the latter's works, and despite Nabokov's great admiration for "The Metamorphosis," the seemingly purposeless sufferings of Cincinnatus in the apparently absurdist world in *Invitation to a Beheading* are transformed into a recapitulation of Gnosticism's cosmic drama of redemption. Contrary to what many critics have claimed, therefore, there is much more to the novel than Nabokov's condemnation of political oppression or his celebration of Cincinnatus's purely imaginative freedom in the face of death. The novel simply cannot be understood without placing the otherworld at the center of its concerns.[4]

Among the numerous evocations of Gnosticism that Davydov has identified and explained in his insightful reading is the central image of Cincinnatus as a prisoner in a labyrinthine stone fortress, which recalls the Gnostic ideas that man is trapped in an evil material world and that his physical body is the prison of his soul. Even such details as the snakelike appearance of the road leading to the fortress and the dog masks the prison guards wear are borrowed from Gnostic symbology of evil. The incident of Cincinnatus walking on air during his childhood, which leads eventually to his imprisonment and death sentence, is modeled on the Gnostic division of mankind into spiritual and fleshly individuals, and on the myth of the original fall of divine spirit into material entrapment. Related to this are such complexes of details as the opposition between Cincinnatus's ethereal appearance and the gross physicality of his wife and his executioner, the image of Cincinnatus stripping off parts of his body as if they were articles of clothing, and his conception of his essential self being like a pearl embedded in a shark's fat – all of which have parallels in Gnostic texts. The Gnostic belief that a savior or a message from the positive, spiritual realm of light can awaken the soul of the chosen individual from its slumberlike state in the darkness of earthly life appears in the novel in such images as the celestial beam that Cincinnatus inexplicably sees piercing a prison corridor, and in the cryptic message that his mother brings him about his mysterious, unknown father. Cincinnatus's oft-repeated but practically incommunicable intuition that he knows something of utmost importance, and his growing recognition that death is to be welcomed as liberation from the earthly prison, reflect the Gnostic idea that salvation is achieved through knowledge of the ultimate truths ("gnosis"). Finally, as Davydov stresses, the destruction of the physical world that follows Cincinnatus's execution and entry into another dimension is a dramatization of the Gnostic belief that upon the return of all spiritual essences to their source in god the material cosmos will be destroyed.[5] Also implicit throughout the novel is the elitism of Gnosticism, according to which Cincinnatus is one of the elect few, and thus certainly not the Everyman some readers take him to be.[6]

Despite the high density of Gnostic details in the novel, *Invitation to a Beheading* is clearly concerned with the same kinds of metaphysical issues we find throughout Nabokov's oeuvre. This is signaled as early as the novel's epigraph, "Comme un fou se croit Dieu, nous nous croyons mortels" (As a madman believes himself to be God, we believe ourselves to be mortal), which is drawn from Pierre Delalande's *Discours sur les ombres*. When unraveled, Delalande's formulation indicates that we are as mistaken to think of ourselves as being mortal as is a madman who thinks he is God – a conclusion that has a clear bearing on Cincinnatus's end as well as on the novel's title. The pointed nature of Nabokov's choice of an epigraph is underscored by the fact that he invented its author, as he admits in the preface to the English translation of the novel (6), and by his readiness to quote from him again, and at much greater length, in an important passage in *The Gift* that also deals with survival after death.

The relevance of the epigraph to the novel is borne out by Cincinnatus's final moments, during which he appears to transcend his mortal being following his decapitation (222–23/217- 18). Nabokov produces this impression through a masterful description of two overlapping series of actions dealing with two Cincinnatuses. The first keeps counting to ten, as the headsman, M'sieur Pierre, instructs him. The second hears the sound of the "unnecessary count" receding after the axe begins to fall, and suddenly experiences a new, joyous insight into his true situation that allows him to get up from the chopping block. The fact that Cincinnatus's mortal self was indeed decapitated during this process is implied by the description of one of the witnesses as sitting "doubled up, vomiting" at the sight. By contrast, the nonphysical nature of the second Cinncinnatus is underscored by the ironic and (in the context) humorous indication that after the axe falls he not only stands up from the block but also *looks* around. This implied duality of body and soul is given an unequivocal ethical coloration when the seemingly "real" setting around the scaffold disintegrates and collapses like a badly constructed stage set. Finally, the novel's concluding phrases, which describe how Cincinnatus "made his way in that direction where, to judge by the voices, stood beings akin to him," imply that he not only survives death but enters a preexisting, and for him, intelligible and familiar transcendent realm.

The dualistic worldview underlying these concluding scenes is repeatedly foreshadowed from the novel's first pages and explains many passages that have either puzzled readers or prompted elaborate, purely metaliterary exegeses (even among those who recognize that the novel's conclusion is couched in imagery implying that Cincinnatus's soul is immortal). For example, the spiritual nature of Cincinnatus's "second" self emerges from the narrator's remarks about the "double" ("prizrak," or "specter" in the original Russian) that he says accompanies everyone – Cincinnatus, himself, and the reader. The explanation that follows reveals how the narrator's claim fits into Nabokov's worldview. The "double"'s distinguishing and highly telling characteristic is that it does "what we would like to do at that very moment, but cannot" (25/37). From this it follows that the second Cincinnatus's leaving the executioner's scaffold after his decapitation is the fullest manifestation of his spiritual being. Moreover, assuming that the "double" is something like a soul that has its true home in a transcendent – which is implied by the second Cincinnatus's going toward "beings akin to him" – imagination can be understood as a function of man's otherworldly nature. Thus in the novel's own terms the "double" is clearly much more than a mere reification of a standard, psychological conception of imagination. This inference is entirely in keeping with what Nabokov implies about the otherworldly dimensions of imagination and inspiration in his discursive writings and recalls what he says in "The Art of Literature and Commonsense" about the anticommonsensical traits of the artistic sensibility.[7]

Additional confirmation for the view that the double is a metaphysical entity in *Invitation to a Beheading* is provided by the narrator's extended digression about the "fleshy incompleteness" of Cincinnatus. Something about him makes it appear "as if one side of his being slid into another dimension"; it also "seemed as though at any moment . . . Cincinnatus would step in such a way as to slip naturally and effortlessly through some chink of the air into its unknown coulisses to disappear there" (120–21/122–24; see also 32/44–45). These descriptions, which imply there is a nonmaterial aspect to Cincinnatus's being, interdict interpretations of his "double" as simple wish fulfillment or as fantasy without foundation in reality. A related feature of the narrator's attempt to characterize Cincinnatus's evanescent nature is his description of him as an unfinished drawing by a "master of masters," which is an impression Cincinnatus also has (21–22/35). Considered outside the context of Nabokov's discursive writings, this passage might appear to warrant a purely metaliterary interpretation of *Invitation to a Beheading*. But, in fact, conceiving of a human being as an artifact is an inevitable consequence of a dualistic worldview in which the transcendent authors the mundane world.

This conclusion is especially important because it underscores the necessity of understanding the novel in the light of Nabokov's Neoplatonic beliefs rather than in exclusively Gnostic terms. The view that spiritual reality rules over matter cannot be reconciled with

Gnosticism's radical dualism, according to which the world of matter is irredeemably evil and separate from the transcendent world of spirit. As a result, one could not liken the implied author of the novel to the hidden, positive god of light in Gnosticism, and see Cincinnatus as his incomplete material creation, because according to Gnostic beliefs the hidden god is not manifested in the material realm in any way other than through the divine spark contained in some select individuals' souls. Cincinnatus's "unfinished" material being would have to be the product of the "demiurge" who rules over the world of fallen matter. In the final analysis, we have to return to the obvious point that although Nabokov may have used Gnostic motifs when it suited him, he did not follow an archaic religious doctrine slavishly.

In the context of the narrator's description of the "double," Cincinnatus's leaving the scaffold after his execution can be seen as the culmination of several earlier flights of the imagination that were incapable of changing his situation permanently. In the second chapter, for example, he drags a table to a window, lifts a chair onto it, and tries unsuccessfully to see out of his cell. Then the jailer appears, and the narrator begins what subsequently turns out to be a deceptive description of how Cincinnatus's double steps on the jailer's face while Cincinnatus himself is getting down from the chair (28–29/40–41). This act is of course a manifestation of Cincinnatus's revulsion at his captivity. More important, however, is the implication that since the jailer is unaware of the full extent of what Cincinnatus's double has done (he sees Cincinnatus climb up but not step on him), the jailer is somehow lacking a "double," or a spiritual faculty with which to register the offense fully. On the other hand, the fact that the jailer can see part of the action carried out by Cincinnatus's double underscores the ontological weight of spiritual reality in the world of the novel (especially for the reader, who is the other witness of Cincinnatus's climb). The deception in the narrator's description of how Cincinnatus's double behaves is signaled by the continuation of the scene. On the following page we find the statement that Cincinnatus "tried – for the hundredth time – to move the table" but could not because "the legs had been bolted down for ages" (30/42). Thus, in light of what we have been told about the nature of the double, the entire incident with Cincinnatus moving the table turns out to be a failed attempt by his spirit to escape its physical confines, against which the corporeal Cincinnatus is also totally impotent. Without this explanation, the narrator's two descriptions of Cincinnatus and the table would appear to be in fundamental contradiction with each other. Thus the novel's metaphysical superstructure preempts any necessity of trying to understand the contradiction in terms of either absurdist or metaliterary criteria.

A second level of deception is implicated here, however, that stems precisely from the fact that there only appears to be a contradiction in the descriptions of Cincinnatus and the table. *Invitation to a Beheading* has built into it several major "flaws" on the level of the narrator's descriptions of events that function as reflections of the novel's central theme, which could be characterized as the imperfection of the material world in comparison to a transcendent prototype. Thus, because the remarks about the table can be reconciled in the novel's own terms, the pseudocontradiction between them can be understood as the narrator's deceptive and elusive strategy of having one device mimic another – a false narrative flaw mimics a real one – which is of course a practice entirely in harmony with the value Nabokov placed on mimicry and deception, as well as with the demands he placed on his readers.[8]

In general, there is a hierarchical arrangement of levels of artifice in the novel, ranging from the fictional world within the text to the reader's interaction with it. The most widespread and obvious form of artifice is based on an extensive elaboration of the metaphor that all the world is a stage. Few readers have failed to notice that Cincinnatus sees himself as being caught in a theatrical performance that does not quite come off even though it supposedly constitutes his real life. For example, the prison director wears a "perfect toupee," has a face "selected without love," and cheeks with a "somewhat obsolete system of wrinkles." He is thus presented as a dated and rather carelessly fashioned simulacrum of a human being. All the other prison personnel are also systematically described in terms of wearing makeup or costumes or of acting, and frequently overacting, their roles (e.g., 21/34, 37/48, 68/76, 78/85, 130/131, 152/152, 210/205).[9]

A somewhat higher level of artifice within the general theatrical motif is defined by flaws in the actual "script" of the "play" being acted out before Cincinnatus. (That he is literally witnessing a play is clearly suggested by the fact that most of the characters who visit him consult crib sheets when they appear to forget their lines.) At one point, M'sieur Pierre tries to entertain Cincinnatus with a trick that involves guessing which card the prison director drew from a deck (84/90). The problem is that Cincinnatus is not included in the "trick," which was ostensibly staged for his benefit, and that no provision was made for verifying that the executioner in fact guessed the correct card. The impression this produces is of a small but significant flaw in the composition or text of the scene, an impression that is confirmed two pages later when M'sieur Pierre tries to repeat the trick but makes a mistake that renders it meaningless (86/93). Under more traditional narrative circumstances, details such as these could be interpreted as simple misunderstandings between the characters. But given the narrator's emphasis on their frequent reliance on crib sheets and the like, the onus for the slips in logic and coherence must fall on the script they continue to follow mechanically without adjusting what they say when their prescribed situations change.

Cincinnatus is well aware that the world surrounding him is a flawed, artificial construct (69–70/77, 91/96), even though he does not notice all the defects. The category of flaws that escapes his notice transcends the relatively untalented acting of the characters around him, as well as the insufficiently polished script they follow, both of which are readily subsumed by the implied consciousness of the text's crafty narrator. This cannot be claimed, however, for the inconsistencies in the novel that simulate flaws on the level of the narrative itself. They are beyond both Cincinnatus's and the narrator's awareness and are thus evidence of the distance between the novel's narrator and its implied author.

A sequence of concealed substitutions of one character for another, which produces the impression that the narrator is forgetting which characters he is dealing with, begins with Cincinnatus's lawyer, Roman Vissarionovich, entering his cell. Next, the prison director, Rodrig Ivanovich, comes in. The two engage in dialogue, until suddenly and without any indication from the narrator that anything is awry, the jailer Rodion, and not the director, appears as the lawyer's interlocutor. This substitution is both marked and masked by the narrator's reference to the interlocutor at one point by the ambiguous term *the former* ("tot" [39/50]) rather than by name. That we are now dealing with Rodion is revealed gradually – first by the reference to his keys, then by his stylized, folksy chatter, and finally by his being addressed by name. An even more elusive instance of the narrator's "forgetfulness" appears in the continuation of this scene, when the lawyer, the jailer, and Cincinnatus go for a walk to a platform at the top of the prison fortress's tower. Cincinnatus stands transfixed by the view, while the lawyer is described as having inadvertently soiled his back with chalk and the jailer sweeps the terrace with a broom he found (43/54). But at the conclusion of the scene the jailer has disappeared, and we read that it is the director, Rodrig Ivanovich, who suddenly tosses away a broom, announces it is time to return inside, and has chalk stains on the back of his coat (44/55).

These shifts, of course, were carefully contrived by Nabokov and are not real slips of the pen. But invoking narrative error is not the only way of interpreting its significance. Later in the novel the narrator acknowledges openly that the director and lawyer look identical without their makeup (207/202). One concludes that the other characters surrounding Cincinnatus may also be interchangeable, which is in fact implied by M'sieur Pierre's ordering the director around at the end of the novel as if he were the jailer (210/205).[10] The reason why characters should be interchangeable can be explained by the novel's metaphysics: If Cincinnatus stands out from among everyone else because he has a soul, it follows that the other characters' identity is most likely the result of their not having souls. Cincinnatus seems aware of this logic, which is why he refers to those around him as "specters, werewolves, parodies" (40/51). However, he gives no sign that he has noticed the specific metamorphosis of the director into the jailer, or vice versa. Of course one character replacing another may be a given in the physical world of *Invitation to a Beheading*, and the narrator may simply be going along with it in the scenes in question. But at the same time he is flaunting a basic fictional convention; moreover, he does so surreptitiously. Thus the absence of any indication in the text that either the narrator or Cincinnatus is aware of the substitutions also makes it possible to interpret them as narrative "errors." Reading them in this way is appealing because the reader is placed in the position of discerning flaws in the text that are analogous to the flaws Cincinnatus perceives in his physical world.[11] Another way of saying this is that Nabokov's simulation of a narrator losing track of characters in his tale – a strikingly original aspect of the novel's aesthetics – is modeled on the novel's metaphysics.

Another link between Nabokov's metaphysical aesthetics and *Invitation to a Beheading* is that Cincinnatus has the gift of what Nabokov called, in *Speak, Memory*, "cosmic synchronization."[12] When Cincinnatus tries to define what makes him unique, he writes in his journal:

> I am not an ordinary – I am the one among you who is alive – Not only are my eyes different, and my hearing, and my sense of taste – not only is my sense of smell like a deer's, my sense of touch like a bat's – but, most important, I have the capacity to conjoin all of this in one point – No, the secret is not revealed yet – even this is but the flint – and I have not even begun to speak of the kindling, of the fire itself. (52/62)

Cincinnatus's reference to his ability to "conjoin" multifarious sensory impressions "in one point" is what sounds most like the epiphanic experience Nabokov knew himself and gave to his favorite characters. Especially telling is that Cincinnatus describes this ability in terms of it being the necessary prerequisite ("the flint") for something much more grand and important ("the fire itself"). One can infer what this is from the context of the passage, which is Cincinnatus's attempt to ameliorate his anguish over not knowing when he will be executed and of his inability to express himself fully in writing (which inextricably links his aesthetic program to his metaphysical quandary). It is vitally important for Cincinnatus to be able to communicate a clarity and immediacy of perception that are like those underlying cosmic synchronization, to make his reader "suddenly feel just as if he had awakened for the first time in a strange country. What I mean to say is that I would make him suddenly burst into tears of joy, his eyes would melt, and, after he experiences this, the world will seem to him cleaner, fresher" (51–52/62). The mention of "awakening," of course, resurrects the motif developed at length in the novel of mundane life as sleep and the transcendent as a true waking state (e.g., 26/39, 36/47, 92/97). A variant of this is the passage dealing with a large, beautiful, and powerful moth – an obvious symbol of the soul[13] – which perceives earthly light in Gnostic terms as a darkness in which it can only "slumber" (203–4/198–99). The view of life in this world as sleep leads readily to Cincinnatus's conclusion that what surrounds him is largely dreamlike and illusory (what he sees during his actual dreams, however, is glimmers of the otherworldly realm [93/99]). It is thus inevitable that he would see the awakening that death brings in terms of a cosmic synchronization-like leap in consciousness.

But why would Cincinnatus think that writing will ameliorate his metaphysical despair? The answer that *Invitation to a Beheading* provides is a variation of Nabokov's metaphysical aesthetics in *Speak, Memory* and "The Art of Literature and Commonsense."

Cincinnatus states that he needs to express himself verbally in order to know the otherworldly reality that fills his intuitions; in other words, poetic language is a guide to, and an expression of, metaphysical reality. This connection is confirmed by Cincinnatus's description of the style he would like to master, which echoes the fire imagery he invokes when speaking of his cosmic synchronization-like gift: "Not knowing how to write, but sensing with my criminal intuition how words are combined, what one must do *for a common-place word to come alive and to share its neighbor's sheen, heat, shadow.* . . . I am nevertheless unable to achieve it, yet that is what is indispensable to me for my task, *a task of not now and not here"* (93/98; emphasis added). Fire imagery also recurs in Cincinnatus's memories of his prenatal origins, an association that establishes yet another link between the otherworld and writing (90/95). Thus we can infer that the fire imagery associated with Cincinnatus's epiphanic sensory acuity, which also underlies his conception of ideally expressive language, is ultimately a reflection of his origins in a cosmic realm. His desire to write is therefore a means of touching that realm through its manifestation in language; it is the existence of that realm that is comforting in the face of physical death. Nabokov traces virtually the same associations among cosmic synchronization, artistic inspiration, and survival after death in "The Art of Literature and Commonsense" when he concludes his characterization of the "inspiration of genius" with the image of the "ego" being liberated from its imprisonment in the world of time and space.[14]

To grasp fully the conception of writing that Nabokov embodies in the novel, it is important to realize that a major discrepancy exists between Cincinnatus's conception of what constitutes ideally expressive language and how he feels he writes himself. Immediately after saying he regrets that he cannot cause his words to share their "sheen, heat, shadow," which he needs, as he puts it in a key phrase, for "netutoshnei moei zadachi" ("my task, a task of not now and not here" – the English translation preserves the *t* alliteration of the Russian), he writes: "Ne tut! Tupoe 'tut,' podpertoe i zapertoe chetoiu 'tverdo,' temnaia tiur'ma, v kotoruiu zakliuchen neuemno voiushchii uzhas, derzhit menia i tesnit" ("Not here! The horrible 'here,' the dark dungeon, in which a relentlessly howling heart is encarcerated, this 'here' holds and constricts me"; 93/98–99). The consonance and assonance in the Russian (especially *t*, but also *o, u, iu, p, zh,* and other sounds) are more prominent than in the English translation and are augmented by the passage's rythmic organization. Furthermore, the repetitions of *t* on the one hand (particularly stressed in the Russian by the phrase "podpertoe i zapertoe chetoiu 'tverdo,'" which is absent altogether from the English and means literally "propped up and locked in by a couple of 'tverdo,'" the old Russian name for the letter *t*), and the word *tut* (here) on the other, acquire additional semantic significance by virtue of their alliterative link to the oft-mentioned Tamara Gardens for which Cincinnatus yearns. The word *tam* means "there" in Russian, which in the context of the novel's oppositions implies not only the freedom of a sylvan setting but also the otherworldly realm that glimmers in Cincinnatus's consciousness and memory.[15] The significance of all these sound repetitions and their associations is that they produce nothing less than an effect *exactly* like that which Cincinnatus holds up as the desirable ideal: each word "reflect[s] itself in its neighbor and renew[s] the neighboring word in the process, so that the whole line is live iridescence" (93/98). Now, the interdependence of sound and meaning is an obvious fact of poetic language, and part of the beauty of Nabokov's Russian and English works stems from the extent to which he exploits alliterative effects. Thus there can be no doubt that the goal Cincinnatus strives to attain and that he achieves unwittingly, has Nabokov's full sanction. But if Cincinnatus is not consciously responsible for what he writes, who is? Could it be his "double," or some other transcendent agency, that guides his hand when he writes beautifully orchestrated prose? One reason this is in fact the most likely explanation is the pressure of the novel's Gnostic context, which makes Cincinnatus's whole existence into an intimate part of a cosmic process. The discrepancy is not just a matter of his being out of touch with his own abilities, therefore, because the novel's metaphysical superstructure provides an explicit, otherworldly explanation for the workings of the "wishful" imagination.

Another reason for invoking an occult force to explain Cincinnatus's writing is that this is the only plausible explanation for an unusual transition that occurs between the narrator's and Cincinnatus's texts, specifically his letter to Marthe in which he tries to convince her that both it and his suffering are real:

[I]t is I, Cincinnatus, who am writing, it is I, Cincinnatus, who am weeping; and who was, in fact, walking around the table, and then, when Rodion brought his dinner, said:

"This letter. This letter I shall ask you to . . . Here is the address . . . "

"You'd do better to learn to knit like everybody else," grumbled Rodion . . . .

"I shall try to ask you anyway," said Cincinnatus, "are there, besides me and that rather obtrusive Pierre, any other prisoners here?"

Rodion flushed but remained silent.

"And the headsman hasn't arrived yet?" asked Cincinnatus.

Rodion was about to furiously slam the already screeching door. (143/143)

The exchanges between Cincinnatus and the jailer continue until M'sieur Pierre arrives, after which the chapter runs on to its end without any explanation of the continuity between Cincinnatus's letter and the narrator's text. This event briefly but significantly changes Cincinnatus's role with regard to the narrator that had been maintained from the start of the novel. After being in a position of relative ignorance, dependence, and passivity in relation to his situation and surroundings, Cincinnatus seems to be suddenly elevated to the privileged position of (relative) omniscience, which is the opposite of the common novelistic practice of having the third-person narrator descend into the more restricted consciousness of a character via free indirect discourse. One way of reconciling the original relation between the two with the apparent change in Cincinnatus's status would be to see him as the narrator's *amanuensis*, both here and by implication elsewhere in the novel. In other words, if one takes the narrator to be something like an occult entity with regard to the characters, then he could be seen as inducing Cincinnatus's thoughts and guiding his writing hand. This could be explained in the novel's own terms by invoking Cincinnatus's "double," which is the side of him that appears attached to a spiritual reality. It would not be reading too much into the text to interpret Cincinnatus's double as occupying the same metaphysical space as the narrator: in a sense, both are free to imagine events that are impossible in "reality." The general agreement between Cincinnatus and the narrator regarding such subjects as the unreality of matter, and the narrator's support for Cincinnatus's nagging intuitions of his spiritual homeland, buttresses the resemblance between them. Moreover, given the narrator's definition of the double, and the fact that Cincinnatus wants to express himself fully in his letter to his wife but feels he does not have the verbal skills necessary to do so, it is appropriate in the novel's terms for his double to try to fulfill this desire. (Another way of saying this is that what Gnosticism would call the "hidden god" manifests himself through Cincinnatus's writing.)

These far-reaching implications of the continuity between Cincinnatus's and the narrator's texts can be reconciled with the "flaws" on the level of the latter by assuming that the narrator "forgot" to indicate a transition from Cincinnatus's letter to his own narrative in the same way that he occasionally "forgets" which characters he is dealing with. If we do not accept the unmarked transition between the narrator's and Cincinnatus's texts as evidence for an occult influence on him, we have to assume that Cincinnatus is in fact the concealed author of the entire novel. The narrative in which he exists would thus be dependent on his consciousness in the same way that his physical world is shown at the novel's conclusion to depend on his mortal existence. Nabokov in fact toys with a similar situation in his short novel *The Eye* (*Sogliadatai*, 1930), where a character's thoughts seem to generate his reality. But such an interpretation of *Invitation to a Beheading* is most implausible because hardly any evidence, beyond that already mentioned, supports it.

Another form of continuity between the narrator's and Cincinnatus's texts which also implies that his writing is literally inspired by an otherworldly agency is, as Davydov argues, that some of his words appear to have been suggested to him directly by the narrator.[16] When Cincinnatus asks to see the catalogue of the prison library, the narrator commiserates about the varieties of "anguish" he must endure (48/58), a word he repeats several more times with a curious insistence (49–50/59–60). Finally Cincinnatus starts setting down his thoughts, and immediately he picks up the word *anguish* and uses it, with the same exclamatory intonation as the narrator, two times near the beginning and two times at the end of his jottings (51/61). It is worth noting that the passage in question includes his description of his sensory acuity, with its implied connection to cosmic synchronization and his awareness of the transcendent. The entire sequence of remarks is thus saturated with intimations of links between Cincinnatus and the otherworld, on the level of both his self-consciousness as well as his lexicon.

Nabokov also creates an oblique link between writing and the otherworld by means of a network of details implying that human life is like a book authored by a transcendent realm. This begins on the second page of *Invitation to a Beheading* when the narrator first compares the waning of Cincinnatus's life to the decreasing thickness of a volume one is reading and then describes a pencil that is "as long as the life of any man except Cincinnatus" (12/26; see also 206/201). The obvious and conventional interpretation of the narrator's remarks is that they are Nabokov's way of calling attention to Cincinnatus's undeniable fictionality. There is, however, a second and more important meaning behind this one. Because the narrator is not merely the teller of Cincinnatus's story but can also be construed as a spiritual entity, his "metaliterary" remarks revaluate Cincinnatus's existence by implying that it is dependent on utterances deriving from the transcendent. What the narrator says is thus doubly deceptive with regard to what he means: not only does Cincinnatus's significance in the novel transcend narrowly metaliterary themes, but because his dualistic nature extends beyond the finitude of earthly life, a book about him that one has finished reading is not an adequate image for the totality of his existence. The implication is that Cincinnatus will continue to exist in some new form after death just as a character continues to "live" in the mind of the reader long after the book in which he appears, and in which he may perish, is set aside. This implicit analogy between text and earthly life, on the one hand, and imagination and the transcendent, on the other, which can be found throughout Nabokov's oeuvre (see especially the deity-like author who induces Krug's saving madness in the conclusion of *Bend Sinister*), is also articulated openly by Cincinnatus when he expresses envy for poets who are able to "speed along a page and, right from the page, where only a shadow continues to run, to take off into the blue" (194/190; a similar formulation appears on 26/38).

The image of a shadow that continues to move while the object casting it has suddenly soared away is a clear adumbration of Cincinnatus's transcending the chopping block at the end of the novel. And if we translate the novel's conclusion back into the terms of Cincinnatus's comments about poetic language, his transcending earthly life puts him into the realm where imagination rules, which, as the narrator's remarks about the "double" suggest, is akin to a spiritual reality. The result of these implications and thematic associations is that the reader, into whose imagination Cincinnatus enters via the act of reading, is placed into the position of an otherworldly witness to Cincinnatus's crossing over into a new form of being. Perhaps one of the meanings of the novel's last phrase about Cincinnatus joining "beings akin to him" is not that he moves into a totally imponderable realm but that his experiences are also the reader's (even if the latter may not have been aware of it). Indeed, part of Nabokov's point in exploiting parallels between elements of fiction and metaphysical beliefs may have been the appeal of confronting the reader with a unique conception of existence by reconceiving the seemingly accessible and familiar act of reading.

Although Cincinnatus appears to be attached to an otherworld, little can be gleaned about it except that it is radically different from earthly life, which is a fundamental aspect of Nabokov's own worldview. It is also entirely in keeping with the radical dualism of Gnosticism, which prohibits easy contact, or even transmission of information, between the material and spiritual realms. One of the most important illustrations of this theme in the novel is the discussion of the bizarre objects called "*nonnons*" by Cecilia C., Cincinnatus's mother. She recalls them from her childhood and is prompted to describe them to him during a visit to his cell after he makes a disparaging remark about the clumsy artificiality of his physical world. She tells him that they appeared shapeless and absurd to normal vision and came with special distorting mirrors in which reflections of everyday objects also made no sense to the eye. But when placed in front of their mirrors, the "*nonnons*" suddenly revealed perfectly intelligible images. Cincinnatus is understandably puzzled as to why his mother would tell him all this, until suddenly, for a brief instant, he sees in her eyes evidence that she knows "that ultimate, secure, all-explaining and from-all-protecting spark that he knew how to discern in himself also. . . . the spark proclaimed such a tumult of truth that Cincinnatus' soul could not help leaping for joy" (135–36/136–38). This is clearly the same divine spark that constitutes both Cincinnatus's soul and his link to the transcendent. The "*nonnons*" thus appear to be models that Cecilia C. invokes (or invents) for the purpose of hinting to Cincinatus that the absurdities and suffering that surround him in prison, which prefigure his impending execution, will show their actual, illusory nature when they are seen in the proper context of the world of spirit. Another way of phrasing this would be to say that one cannot imagine the true shape of the experiences one may have on the other side of the division between this world and the next.

Although the otherworld may be ultimately unfathomable, Cincinnatus's experience of time constitutes another nexus of themes and images that sheds light on the relation between the material and spiritual planes of being. On the one hand, he describes how he once saw a man move away from a wall while his shadow seemed briefly to remain behind: "Between his movement and the movement of the laggard shadow – that second, that syncope – there is the rare kind of time in which I live" (53/63). And in the next sentence Cincinnatus goes on to intimate that he is attached by an "invisible umbilical cord" to a mysterious otherworldly realm. The two remarks support each other by implying that Cincinnatus's proper environment, or, more exactly, that of his double, is both timeless and spiritual. On the other hand, he is also a physical being, which is why his mundane life is characterized not by timelessness but by a dulling, repetitive cyclicity that is a function of a prison's inevitable routine. This is reinforced by such details as his discovering that a prison corridor circles back to his cell (77/84) and that the tunnel M'sieur Pierre had dug leads to the prison director's quarters (166/165). Cincinnatus's attempt to characterize the atemporal "moment" in which he lives anticipates the imagery Van Veen will use in his discussion of time in *Ada*, which in turn reflects Nabokov's own beliefs.[17] Cincinnatus also anticipates Nabokov's deceptive description in *Speak, Memory* of time as a spherical prison when he says that "the sphere of my own self still limits and eclipses my being" ["soboiu oblo ogranichen i zatmen"] (89–90/95). There is a resemblance as well between the ways Cincinnatus and Nabokov escape these prisons. After he leaves the scaffold Cincinnatus is described as being "overtaken by Roman, who was now many times smaller" (222–23/217), which suggests that Cincinnatus has grown or expanded beyond the limits of his old, corporeal self. A radically expanded consciousness that appears to be capable of embracing all existence is also part of Nabokov's repertoire of images in *Speak, Memory* when he describes the timeless moment of cosmic synchronization.

Time is inevitably central to Cincinnatus's ceaseless attempts to determine when he will be executed. That he consistently fails to guess the answer or to cajole it from various visitors to his cell may be a reflection of Nabokov's idea that one's future is unknowable or that it does not exist because it is not fixed, at least for mortal consciousness. The latter qualification needs to be added because of a detail in the scene between Cincinnatus and his mother. Immediately after he notices the spark in her gaze that causes his heart to leap for joy, the narrator describes Cecilia C. as making an "incredible little gesture": she "hold[s] her hands apart with index fingers extended, as if indicating size – the length, say, of a babe" (136/138). Although the narrator underscores the significance of the mother's cryptic gesture, he leaves it to the reader to interpret it. The sequence of events in this scene suggests that, on one level, the gesture may be the mother's indication of how little time her son has left to live; on another level, however, it can be interpreted as indicating that he has to wait only a little while longer before all mysteries are revealed. The latter is implied by the narrator's reference to a "babe," which, from the context, emerges as a veiled hint about death as a rebirth. Cincinnatus does not seem even to notice his mother's gesture, much less try to understand it, which suggests it is his double, rather than his not fully conscious mortal self, that rejoices at recognizing the spark. But his relative purblindness does not negate the evidence that Cecilia C.'s role in the novel is that of a Gnostic more "advanced" than he is. She not only possesses the divine spark but seems able to reveal it at will; she knows that Cincinnatus's father was also a "pneumatic" or spiritual being; and, by describing the "*nonnons*," she implies that she understands the ultimate mysteries of existence, such as the irreconcilable difference between the Gnostic worlds of matter and spirit. One concludes, therefore, that from her superior vantage point Cincinnatus's future may not be a secret. As a result, Cincinnatus emerges as having been wrong to accuse her of being a "parody" (132/133), a point Nabokov implied himself in an interview when he said that Cincinnatus's accusation was not quite fair.[18]

The links among Cincinnatus's perceptions, his verbal creation, and his otherworldly origins point up another major difference between Gnosticism's dualism and Nabokov's beliefs. Cincinnatus resembles his creator in that his sensory acuity bespeaks an attraction to, and an understanding of, the things of this world. Even though Cincinnatus sees through the shabby artifice that characterizes the man-made and human realms around him, he still loves his shallow, grossly physical, and cruelly unfaithful wife (60/69), yearns for the Tamara Gardens where he used to roam (27–28/40), and even longs for scenes of street life in town (73–75/80–82). In other words, his attitude toward aspects of the physical world is not consistently negative, as Gnosticism would require. One could argue that Cincinnatus overcomes these feelings by the end of the novel, when his spiritual side manages to gain greater ascendancy over the physical. He suggests as much himself when he writes that he has reached "the dead end of this life, and I should not have sought salvation within its confines" (205/200). But just before M'sieur Pierre finally arrives to convey Cincinnatus to the place of execution, we are presented with the second extended description of the moth that had escaped the jailer. The passage is thus located at a crucial juncture in the text. It is typically Nabokovian not only by virtue of its subject matter but also in the way the moth's physical attributes are described in great detail, and in the general tone of admiration that surrounds the insect's combined beauty and power. The moth's traditional significance as a symbol of the soul is overt, and the eyespots on its wings evoke one of Nabokov's favorite images for the all-embracing consciousness that man may achieve after death (in *The Gift*, Delalande will specu-late that after death man will become an "all-seeing eye"). In his enchantment Cincinnatus strokes the moth's large wings, which prompts the narrator to exclaim, "what gentle firmness! what un-yielding gentleness!" The importance of this characterization is that it reminds the reader of the implausibility of the jailer's plan to feed the moth to the spider, which is an equally obvious symbol of death. (The spider's emergence as artificial [78/85, 210/205] is of course yet another suggestion that death is illusory.) Because the passage is narrated in free indirect discourse, Cincinnatus is implicated in the entire loving description of the magnificent insect, which is a point of view at odds not only with his own general denigration of the physical world but with Gnosticism's attitude toward it. (Similarly, Nabokov grants Cincinnatus another of his favorite gifts – skill at chess [144/146].) The possibility that Cincinnatus's involuntary at-traction to the moth is a reflection of Nabokov's disagreement with Gnosticism – and therefore his way of correcting the overly spiritu-alized view that his protagonist developed – is also suggested by Cincinnatus's error regarding his mother in the passage preceding the description of the moth. He had included "a mother's moist gaze" in the list of "theatrical, pathetic" things that had "duped" him and that motivated his conviction that "salvation" must not be sought on earth. Cincinnatus thus appears to have forgotten his own (or not registered his double's) exultant recognition of the truth of what she told him and of the spiritual spark both share. Nabokov's ability to capture sensuous details, which is one of the most striking and oft-celebrated features of his writing from both his Russian and English periods, did not prevent him from being able to transcend matter via matter, as it were, in his conception of cosmic synchronization and in his views on mimicry and artifice in nature. The difference between Nabokov's views and Cincinnatus's partially Gnostic attitudes toward matter could thus be described as relative – one of degree and tone – not substantive.

––––––

The connection between ethics and metaphysics in *Invitation to a Beheading* is one of the most obvious and straightforward in Nabokov's oeuvre. Good is firmly attached to Cincinnatus because he is the only character (except for his mother) who has intimations of, and spiritual links to, a transcendent realm; this insight is what allows him to see the physical world for what it is. The other characters are totally ignorant of this higher realm; as a result, they are mired in a shallow physical world and are consistently presented as foolish, absurd, and irredeemably vulgar. M'sieur Pierre is an especially perfect embodiment of that petty evil or self-satisfied vulgarity called "*poshlost'*" in Russian to which Nabokov gave famous definition in his book on Gogol. Cincinnatus's Platonic love for Marthe is in stark contrast to her grossly carnal sexuality, which Nabokov renders with striking mastery (141/142). The failing of these and other characters is pointed up by Cincinnatus's overwhelming desire to make them understand his plight, something they are constitutionally incapable of doing. There is, however, no horrible or Satanic evil in the novel, which reflects Nabokov's own view of evil as absence and thus constitutes an additional departure from Gnostic dualism.

The dominant theatrical metaphor that Cincinnatus and the narrator use in describing the world in the novel adds aesthetics to the continuum between ethics and metaphysics. Both have grasped that matter is an imperfect copy, or a lesser image, of a spiritual reality (a belief also at odds with Gnosticism). But since gnosis is the province of the few, the values embodied in *Invitation to a Beheading*, as in all of Nabokov's other works, emerge as inflexibly elitist. The only character who will be saved is Cincinnatus (and perhaps his mother; the ambiguous image in the novel's final paragraph of "a woman in a black shawl, carrying the tiny executioner like a larva in her arms" may be Cecilia C.). All the other characters are automatons for whom even the category of salvation is irrelevant. In connection with this, it is interesting that Cincinnatus implies that children have the potential to develop into something better than what most adults become in his fallen world and that he was closer to the transcendent himself when he was a child (95/100–101). This anticipates Nabokov's own conception of his son's childhood in *Speak, Memory*, which is characterized by hints of links to transmundane modes of being. It also harkens back to widespread Romantic and Symbolist topoi embodied in such works as Wordsworth's ode "Intimations of Immortality from Recollections of Early Childhood" and Andrei Bely's novel *Kotik Letaev*. Indeed, Nabokov's art has definite affinities with both of these works and movements.

NOTES

1. For more on this see my *Nabokov's Otherworld* (Princeton, N.J.: Princeton University Press, 1991), 1–22, 235–36. The present article is a shortened version of chapter 3 from this book, which is reprinted with permission from Princeton University Press. See also my "The Otherworld" and "Nature and Artifice" in *The Garland Companion to Vladimir Nabokov*, ed. Vladimir E. Alexandrov (New York: Garland, 1995), 553–56, 566–71.

2. Hereafter, all page references to the 1989 Vintage International reprint of the English translation, and the Paris: Editions Victor, n.d., reprint of the Russian, will be given in the text in the following form: (English page number / Russian page number). The allegorical character of the novel was noted by Bitsilli as soon as it appeared in an émigré journal; see "The Revival of Allegory," in *Nabokov: Criticism, Reminiscences, Translations and Tributes*, ed. Alfred Appel, Jr., and Charles Newman (Evanston, Ill.: Northwestern University Press, 1971), 102–18.

3. Julian Moynahan, "Predislovie," *Priglashenie na kazn'* (1938; rpt. Paris: Editions Victor, n.d.), 13–17; "A Russian Preface for Nabokov's *Beheading*," *Novel* 1 (1967): 12–18. Sergej Davydov, *"Teksty-Matreški" Vladimira Nabokova* (Munich: Otto Sagner, 1982), 100–182; and *"Invitation to a Beheading*," in *The Garland Companion*, 188–203. See also Jonathan Borden Sisson, "Cosmic Synchronization and Other Worlds in the Work of Vladimir Nabokov," Ph.D. diss., University of Minnesota, 1979, 140–41, for a discussion of the novel as an "elaboration of the themes of H. G. Wells's 'The Country of the Blind'"; however, Sisson does not claim any parallels based on otherworldly thematics.

4. More criticism has been published on *Invitation to a Beheading* than on any of Nabokov's Russian novels. The earliest and most famous reading of the novel as a quintessentially metaliterary work is Vladislav Khodasevich's essay "On Sirin" (1937); see the partial translation by Michael H. Walker, edited by Simon Karlinsky and Robert P. Hughes, in *Nabokov: Criticism, Reminiscences, Translations and Tributes*, ed. Alfred Appel, Jr., and Charles Newman, 96–101. (A rare disagreement with Khodasevich's influential views from within the emigration is Vladimir Varshavskii, *Nezamechennoe pokolenie* [New York: Chekhov, 1956], 215, 223.)

For a contemporary American reading, see Julian W. Connolly, "Nabokov's 'Terra Incognita' and 'Invitation to a Beheading': The Struggle for Imaginative Freedom," *Wiener Slawistischer Almanach* 12 (1983): 55–65. The reluctance of some critics to accept the novel's metaphysical dimension is well illustrated by Dick Penner, "Invitation to a Beheading: Nabokov's Absurdist Initiation," *Critique: Studies in Modern Fiction* 20.3 (1979), who concludes that the novel is "a classic work of absurdist literature" (33). Similarly Margaret Byrd Boegeman, *"Invitation to a Beheading* and the Many Shades of Kafka," in *Nabokov's Fifth Arc*, ed. J. E. Rivers and Charles Nicol (Austin: University of Texas Press, 1982), denies the novel any "spiritual" or "ethical" concern and tries to present it as Nabokov's exhortation to himself to switch to English (see page 112). For a subtle and careful investigation of Nabokov's relation to Kafka, see John Burt Foster, Jr., *Nabokov's Art of Memory and European Modernism* (Princeton, N.J.: Princeton Uniersity Press, 1993), 15–16; and "Nabokov and Kafka," in *The Garland Companion*, 444–51. Andrew Field, *VN: The Art and Life of Vladimir Nabokov* (New York: Crown, 1986), sees the novel as "triumphant solipsism" (150). Dale E. Peterson, "Nabokov's *Invitation*: Literature as Execution," *PMLA* 96.5 (1981): 824–36 (reprinted in the present volume), recognizes that the novel supports a metaphysical reading but returns to a view of Nabokov as a metaliterary writer opposed to "realism." David Rampton, *Vladimir Nabokov: A Critical Study of the Novels* (Cambridge: Cambridge University Press, 1984), sees Cincinnatus as finding himself "in a fallen world" (40-41). Robert Alter, "*Invitation to a Beheading*: Nabokov and the Art of Politics," in *Nabokov: Criticism, Reminiscences, Translations and Tributes* (reprinted in the present volume), speaks of Nabokov's "aesthetic" as leading back "to a metaphysic, and one with ultimately moral implications" (55), but he means something quite different by these terms than I do: he concludes that the novel is concerned with dramatizing that the "inevitability of [the artist's] partial failure spur[s] him to attempt again and again the impossible magic of comprehending life in art" (58). By contrast, Brian Boyd, *Vladimir Nabokov: The Russian Years* (Princeton, N.J.: Princeton University Press, 1990), reads the novel in terms congruent with my own (see 410-17); and Julian W. Connolly, *Nabokov's Early Fiction: Patterns of Self and Other* (Cambridge: Cambridge University Press, 1992), examines the protagonist's self-transcendence in terms that can also be correlated with a metaphysical reading of the novel (166-84).

5. Davydov, "*Teksty-Matreški*," 112-14, 117-23, 128-32, 133-40. Motifs congruent with Gnostic myth, but not necessarily derived from it, can also be found in Nabokov's poetry of the 1920s. See, for example, "O, kak ty rvesh'sia v put' krylatyi" (1923; Oh how you strain to be on [your] winged way), in *Stikhi* (Ann Arbor: Ardis, 1979), 103. As Nabokov indicated himself in his Introduction to *Bend Sinister* (New York: Vintage International, 1990), xii, there are strong parallels between it and *Invitation to a Beheading*.

6. For example, Bitsilli, "The Revival of Allegory," 116; and Alter, "*Invitation*," 58.

7. For more on this, see *Nabokov's Otherworld*, 53-57.

8. See ibid., 45-46.

9. The theatrical theme has been noted widely; see, for example, Dabney Stuart, *Nabokov: The Dimensions of Parody* (Baton Rouge: Louisiana State University Press, 1978), 58-66; and Ellen Pifer, *Nabokov and the Novel* (Cambridge, Mass.: Harvard University Press, 1980), 49-67.

10. Stuart discusses other interchangeable characters (*Nabokov*, 61-62).

11. Stuart makes a similar point but to a radically different end, namely, that imagination can triumph over limitations placed on it (*Nabokov*, 71).

12. See *Nabokov's Otherworld*, 26-29.

13. The symbolic function of the moth is not vitiated by the assertion Nabokov made in an interview: "That in some cases [i.e., paintings by Old Masters] the butterfly symbolizes something (e.g., Psyche) lies utterly outside my area of interest" (*Strong Opinions* [New York: Vintage International, 1990], 168). Nabokov uses a large moth as an overt symbol of a dead boy's immortal soul in the short story "Rozhdestvo" (1925), translated as "Christmas."

14. *Lectures on Literature* (New York: Harcourt Brace Jovanovich / Bruccoli Clark, 1980), 378.

15. D. Barton Johnson, *Worlds in Regression: Some Novels of Vladimir Nabokov* (Ann Arbor, Mich.: Ardis, 1985), discusses various motifs related to letters of the alphabet (28–32); see also pages 157–164 for an analysis of the novel's "two world" theme.

16. Davydov, *"Teksty-Matreški"*, 150–51.

17. Van Veen discusses at length the nature of time and his disbelief in the future in *Ada*, part 4. In *Strong Opinions*, Nabokov suggests that he shares some of Van's essential views on the subject (see 185–86).

18. Nabokov, *Strong Opinions*, 76. David Rampton makes a similar point; see *Vladimir Nabokov: A Critical Study of the Novels*, 59–60. By contrast, Susan Strehle Klemtner argues that Cecilia C.'s lesson to her son is that he "can be reborn if he will abandon fixed space for a fluid, moving angle of vision"; see "To 'Special Space': Transformotion in *Invitation to a Beheading*," *Modern Fiction Studies* 25.3 (1979): 436.

The Alpha and Omega of
Nabokov's *Invitation to a Beheading*

D. BARTON JOHNSON

Nabokov is a man of letters in the most literal sense of the term.[1] In his autobiographies, *Speak, Memory* and *Drugie berega*, Nabokov notes that the childhood discovery of his own alphabetic chromesthesia ("colored hearing") came about when he observed to his mother that the colored letters on his new set of wooden alphabet blocks were "wrong."[2] Each letter/sound of the alphabet involuntarily evoked a specific and constant color for him. Nabokov then details the color-sound-letter correspondences for each symbol of the Russian and English alphabets. In consequence, every word has its own color sequence. In Nabokov's Russian pen name "СИРИН" (Sirin), referring to a brightly colored mythological bird, the Cyrillic letter/sound С (s) is brilliant light blue; the И (i), golden; the Р (r) sound, a wriggly black; and the Н (n), yellow.[3] So enchanted was Nabokov by this psychological phenomenon that he used it to devise an elaborate metaphor for his art, even coining nonce "rainbow" words that emblematize his creative processes in Russian and English. From the Russian letters evoking red, orange, yellow, green, blue, indigo, and violet, he coined the rainbow word ВЁЕПСКЗ (*V-Yo-Ye-P-S-K-Z*), corresponding to the English schoolboy mnemonic acronym ROY G. BIV; for his English rainbow term, he devised the "word" *KZSPYGV*. The oddity is that the English rainbow word reflects a backward or mirror-image spectrum, for example, violet, indigo, . . . red.

The explanation for this reversal is found in nature. The rainbow we commonly see is called a "primary" rainbow. On rare occasions we also see a larger, fainter "secondary" rainbow just above the primary rainbow, but with the order of the colors reversed. Nabokov has drawn on his alphabetic chromesthesia, the source of the Russian and English rainbow "words," to emblematize his creation in Russian, his "primary" language, and in English, his "secondary" tongue. This emblem serves not only to signify the major theme of his autobiography – his creative life – but also as a unifying master metaphor that gathers into itself many of the book's secondary motifs: the colored pencils, the stained-glass window panes, the multicolored imperial illuminations, his mother's jewels, and so on.[4]

Individual letters may depict visual images as well as collectively constituting meaningful words. If letter colors were the central device for indicating the theme of Nabokov's autobiography, letter shapes play this role in his Russian novel *Invitation to a Beheading*. This dystopian work is set in a nameless, nightmarish state of the future – a fantasized Russia circa the year 3000.[5] Apart from the initial courtroom scene, the bizarre gala dinner, and the final execution scene, the entire novel takes place in the prison-fortress where the protagonist, Cincinnatus, attended by his jailers and his executioner, awaits the unknown day of his beheading.[6] Cincinnatus's crime is "gnostical turpitude," the perception and knowledge of forbidden things in a world where all things are already known and named.[7] Overtly, Cincinnatus's criminality takes the form of being opaque in a society whose citizens are all transparent, devoid of fresh perceptions, lacking dark corners in their minds or souls, people with no secret from one another.

Cincinnatus, alone in this world, has intimations of another world, one "alive . . . captivatingly majestic, free and ethereal" (92/97).[8] The novel's thematic structure is cast in terms of the opposition of these two worlds, the "real" world of Cincinnatus's intuitions, a world he feels to be far more real than that in which he awaits death. Much of the novel centers around Cincinnatus's mental probing of this ideal world and his vain efforts to find verbal means of expressing its reality both to himself and others. The novel as a whole is permeated by an alphabetic motif, and the central theme of

Cincinnatus's struggle to realize and convey his insight is specifically associated with the device of alphabetic iconicism.

The very origin of Cincinnatus's awareness of his differentness from his fellows, of his inherent criminality, is linked with alphabetic symbols. Thinking back to his childhood, he recalls: "Well do I remember that day! I must have just learned how to make letters, since I remember myself wearing on my fifth finger the little copper ring that was given to children who already knew how to copy the model words from the flower beds in the school garden, where petunias, phlox and marigold spelled out lengthy adages" (96/101). The acquisition of letters marks the end of the protagonist's innocence.

The letter motif figures in a minor way on several occasions. In examining an old volume from the prison library, Cincinnatus wonders "in what language is this written. The small, crowded, ornate type, with dots and squiggles within the sickle-shaped letters, seemed to be oriental – it was somehow reminiscent of the inscriptions on museum daggers" (125/127). Elsewhere we are told that a "drop of water had fallen on the page. Through the drop several letters turned from brevier to pica, having swollen as if a reading glass had been lying over them" (88/94). The prison library also provides Cincinnatus with a copy of the novel *Quercus* where he finds "a paragraph a page and a half long in which all the words begin with 'p'" (123/125). The letter motif also finds expression in references to monograms and handwriting. Such is the mention of an "alligator album with its massive dark silver monogram" (169/168) and of Pierre, the executioner, whose handwriting is characterized as "fleecily curling script, elegant punctuation marks, [and] signature like a seven veiled dance" (118/120).[9] A more pointed occurrence of the letter motif is its use to designate the particular kindergarten division in which Cincinnatus teaches. In view of his doubtful reliability he is permitted to work only with the physically defective in division "Φ" ("F") (30/42). One of the old letter names for the Cyrillic Φ was *fita* which has the secondary meaning "one who is useless or superfluous."[10] These and still other references fall into the category of more or less incidental ornamentation with the function of keeping the alphabetic motif before the reader's eye.

A different dimension in the use of alphabetic devices is represented by a number of cases in which each usage is associated with the novel's theme at key points in the book's structure. Some pertain to aspects of character and plot; others, to theme. Cincinnatus's death cell is adjacent to a cell occupied by one Pierre whose job it is first to befriend Cincinnatus and then to behead him. Pierre is a paradigm of his totalitarian world whose denizens are banally trivial. He stands in opposition to Cincinnatus whose intimations of a different world and another mode of being convict him of a capital crime. The two coeval characters are contrastively paired in many senses. Cincinnatus is delicate, slender, and neurasthenic, whereas Pierre is robust, plump, and jolly: deep integrity/shallow vulgarity; artist/philistine; victim/executioner. This pairing comes to a head at the preexecution gala dinner party at which Cincinnatus and Pierre are guests of honor. After the meal the guests go out into the night to view the execution eve festive illumination:

> For three minutes a good million light bulbs of diverse colors burned, artfully planted in the grass, in branches, on cliffs, and all arranged in such a way as to embrace the whole nocturnal landscape with a grandiose monogram of "P" and "C," which, however, had not quite come off. (189)

The paired initials are, of course, those of Pierre and Cincinatus, but the English text loses an important instance of the alphabetic iconicism conveyed by the Russian, where the "grandiose monogram" consists of П and Ц. The Russian letters are almost, but not quite, perfect upside-down mirror images of each other. Note also that the alphabetic symbol for the odious Pierre stands with feet on the ground and closed off to the sky at the top; conversely, Cincinnatus's symbol is open to a world above. This is not the end of the matter. Nabokov calls attention to his device by specifically noting that the monogrammed pair "had not quite come off." By alluding to the small tail hanging from Cincinnatus's Ц, Nabokov calls attention to the graphic symbolism of the contrasting characters. The letter shapes mirror the opposition of the two chief characters. This effect is largely lost in the English translation where the physically dissimilar initials *P* and *C* can link but cannot iconically oppose Pierre and Cincinnatus.

The above example draws on the physical shape of the monogrammatic letters to emblematize the oppositional relationship between the two main characters and, through them, the two worlds of the novel. As we have said, this binary opposition that is manifested throughout the book serves as an organizing context for the novel's central theme. Cincinnatus, awaiting the fall of the axe, feels a compulsion to communicate his vague sense of another world via his prison journal, to leave a record, a legacy against that day when someone might understand and benefit. Only Cincinnatus can convey the truth of that dimly glimpsed world for "I am the one among you who is alive. Not only are my eyes different, and my hearing, and my sense of taste – not only is my sense of smell like a deer's, my sense of touch like a bat's – but most important, I have the capacity to conjoin all this in one point." (52/62). The English translation fails to convey an important nuance here in that the word *capacity* replaces the Russian *dar* in the sense of an innate talent, that is, a "gift." This is important, for it is by this word that Cincinnatus identifies himself as an artist. He goes on to assert that, if granted time, he would write "about how part of my thoughts is always crowding around the invisible umbilical cord that joins this world to something – to what I shall not say yet" (53/63).

In spite of Cincinnatus's initial assurance in his secret knowledge and in his "capacity/gift" of expression, this task proves to be enormously difficult and, in the context of the novel's world, ultimately impossible. His struggle to convey his vision, to express the *other* world in the terms of *this* world, is the novel's thematic focal point. Cincinnatus's prison, as much else in the novel, is double. He awaits death in the prison fortress of the totalitarian state and, more important thematically, in the prison-house of language.[11] The one is the usual place of repose for the political and intellectual dissident; the other, that of the verbal artist. Just as Cincinnatus's attempts to escape his physical prison are circuitously hopeless so are his efforts to break through the walls of the prison-house of language. The theme of attempting to express the inexpressible is explicitly discussed in several passages in *Invitation to a Beheading*. It is precisely and exclusively in conjunction with these passages that a special sort of alphabetic iconicism is cunningly interwoven into the text.

The prison-house of language theme has two interrelated aspects: the artist's restricted capacity to convey his vision in the existing language and his audience's inability to understand even that which can be expressed. We shall first examine a passage addressing the latter aspect. Cincinnatus is first denounced for opacity while still a child. Throughout his youth he tries to learn to mimic the transparency of his fellow beings, but he cannot wholly succeed: "Those around him understood each other at the first word, since they had no words that would end in an unexpected way, perhaps in some archaic letter, an upsilamba, becoming a bird or a catapult[12] with wondrous consequences" (26/38). The passage goes on to say that in the dusty town museum that Cincinnatus often visited were many "rare marvelous objects, but all of the townsmen except Cincinnatus found them just as limited and transparent as they did each other. *That which does not have a name does not exist. Unfortunately everything had a name*" (26/38).[13]

This is a succinct statement of the prison-house of language theme. The artist's potential audience cannot comprehend his message for their language is hermetic. All things are named and the nameless cannot even be conceived of, much less exist. On the other hand, the recognized universe, narrow and banal as it may be, is immediately and easily accessible to all. Speakers of the received tongue understand each other "at the first word." The only way new meanings or insights might be imparted would be by the introduction of an additional alphabetic symbol. In illustration, Nabokov creates a new hybrid letter, an "upsilamba," rather than using an archaic one. It is archaic only in the sense that the coined name represents a blending of the ancient Greek "upsilon" (Υ, υ) and the "lambda" (Λ, λ), the former indeed resembling the head-on view of a bird in flight and the latter an (inverted) slingshot. Both the letter shapes and the tropes are suggestive of Cincinnatus's desire that his imprisoned words (as well as his person) take flight, that he might succeed in communicating with others.

Comparison of the above passage with Nabokov's Russian text once again reveals the loss of a significant thematic element. Rather than the "upsilon" plus "lambda" hybrid, he proposes restoration of a missing final letter that might let words take flight – an "*izhitsa*" (V), the last character of the Old Church Slavonic alphabet, the thousand-year-old liturgical script of the Slavic peoples. Although the modern Russian alphabet is derived from the Church Slavonic (which in turn is largely derived from the Greek), the *izhitsa* (V) has long since been abandoned. Note that this letter also resembles the bird and catapult images, but more important, it calls attention to a theological and, as we shall see, structural meaning of the novel's alphabetic icons.

As noted above, in the case of the mirror-image monograms of Pierre and Cincinnatus, the switch of alphabets from Russian to English resulted in the loss of an important detail serving to rein-force the book's thematic basic dichotomy. This is even more so in the example at hand. The letter name *izhitsa* is useless for the English translation since the English reader does not know the charac-ter's shape (V). Nabokov attempts to surmount this in the English version by drawing on the Greek alphabet and creating the hybrid compound "upsilamba." Thus he has solved the *izhitsa* translation problem in an ingenious way. It should be noted, however, that just as Russian readers, if they are to grasp the allusive imagery, must know (and apply) the iconic shape of the Church Slavonic *izhitsa*, English-speaking readers must be familiar with the Greek alphabet – perhaps not an altogether realistic expectation.

The prison-house of language theme is resumed in chapter 8 when Cincinnatus meditates on his knowledge of a realm forbidden and inaccessible to others: "I know something. But the expression of it comes so hard" (91/96).[14] In his prison journal he records his fears: "[N]othing [will] come of what I am trying to tell, its only vestiges being the corpses of strangled words, like hanged men . . . evening silhouettes of gammas and gerunds, gallow crows" (90/96). The Greek gamma (Γ) of the English text does convey the silhouettes of the gallows or, more exactly, that of the gibbet from which the corpses of Cincinnatus's strangled words will hang. The iconic image is all the more effective in that it evokes Cincinnatus's imminent execution, although it is to be by the axe rather than the rope. The English version of this alphabetic icon is handled in the same way as in the preceding case – by conversion of the Church Slavonic letter into its identically shaped Greek equivalent, the letter gamma.

Here, once again, the thematic subtext is lost in translation. The Russian text ends in the words *glagol'* and *voron'e* (96) where the English has "gammas and gerunds, gallow crows" (90). In an effort to relay the full effect of the Russian, Nabokov has added the alliterative "gerunds" and "gallow." The first is an ingenious but not wholly successful attempt to find a parallel to the second meaning of *glagol'*. In addition to being the proper name for the Church Slavonic letter Γ, *glagol'* is nearly identical with the Church Slavonic word *glagol* meaning "word." This is uniquely appropriate here since "strangled words" are the sole remnants of Cincinnatus's vision. "Gallow crows" is offered as a translation for the Russian *voron'e* which is simply a group of crows. Nabokov's insertion of "gallows" calls the reader's attention to the alphabetic imagery of the Greek letter "gamma" (Γ), that is, its resemblance to a gallows. As an aside, it might be remarked that the shape of the Greek "gamma" is, strictly speaking, that of the single-armed gibbet rather than that of the gallows which has two uprights surmounted by a cross bar. The latter finds its most apt alphabetic icon in the Cyrillic П, which, coincidentally, is the initial of Pierre, Cincinnatus's executioner.

The principal way in which the thematic dichotomy of "this world /that world" is maintained throughout the novel is through the recurrent contrast of the Russian deictic terms *tut* (pronounced "toot"), "here," and *tam* (pronounced "Tom"), "there." This particular manifestation of the opposition is most intensively and explicitly elaborated in chapter 8, which consists entirely of an extract from Cincinnatus's prison journal. It is in this section that Cincinnatus most directly confronts the problem of trying to convey his vision of a true reality (*tam*) in the context and language of the oppressive world of the prison (*tut*).[15]

In his journal Cincinnatus struggles to describe his "soul's native realm," that is, "that world" (there) versus "this world" (here). Despite his difficulties he feels himself on the brink of success, saying, "I think I have caught my prey . . . but it is only a fleeting apparition of my prey!" (94/99). The passage continues:

> Tam – nepodrazhaemoi razumnost'iu svetitsia chelovecheskii vzgliad; tam na vole guliaiut umuchennye tut chudaki; tam vremia skliadyvaetsia po zhelaniiu. . . . Tam, tam – original tekh sadov, gde my tut brodili, skryvalis'; tam vse porazhaet svoeiu charuiushchei ochevidnost'iu, prostotoi sovershennogo blaga; tam vse poteshaet dushu. (99–100)

> *There, tam, là-bas*, the gaze of men glows with inimitable understanding; *there* the freaks that are tortured here walk unmolested; *there* time takes shape according one's pleasure. . . . *There, there* are the originals of those gardens where we used to roam and hide in this world; *there* everything strikes one by its bewitching evidence, by the simplicity of perfect good; *there* everything pleases one's soul.[16] (94)

In spite of the intensity of his vision and his desire to express it, Cincinnatus cannot achieve his goal:

> Not knowing how to write, but sensing with my criminal intuition how words are combined, what one must do for a commonplace word to come alive and share its neighbor's sheen, heat, shadow, while reflecting itself and its neighbor and renewing the neighboring word in the process, so that the whole line is live irides-

cence; while I sense the nature of this word propinquity, I am nevertheless unable to achieve it, yet that is what is indispensable to me for my task, a task of not now and not here. (93/98)

This last phrase leads Cincinnatus into a remarkable passage built around the Russian word *tut* (here) which is counterposed to the *tam* passage above:

Ne tut! Tupoe "tut" podpertoe i zapertoe chetoiu "tverdo," temnaia tiur'ma, v kotoruiu zakliuchen neuemno voiushchii uzhas, derzhit menia i tesnit. (98–99)

_____

Not here! The obtuse *tut* (here) propped up and locked in by its pair of *T*s, the dark dungeon in which a relentlessly howling "uuu" of horror is entombed, confines me and restricts. [My translation – D.B.J.; see page 93 for Nabokov's.]

The two passages cited here and above afford the most obvious juxtaposition and explicit rendering of the oppositional pair *tut/tam*. It is not by chance that both passages are presented within the context of the prison-house of language theme. Cincinnatus cannot escape from the world of "here" into the world of "there" even though he doubts the reality of the former. He is incarcerated in the prison-house of language just as surely as he is in the prison fortress. We have shown that the use of alphabetic iconicism is closely associated with this theme, and we shall show that this is even more spectacularly the case in the passage at hand. Before doing so, however, I would like to comment on the phonetic symbolism of a part of the passage. If we reexamine the first part of the sentence, that is, "*Ne Tut! Tupoe 'TuT' podperToe i zaperToe cheToiu 'Tverdo'. . . ,*" we see that the entire phrase is phonetically built on a series of *T* alliterations that take their origin from the key word *tut*. Further, the latter half of the sentence, that is, "*Temnaia Tiur'ma, v koTorUiU zakliUchen neUemno voiUshchii Uzhas, derzhiT menia i TesniT,*" is structured on the phonetic framework *TTTUUUUUUTTT* with its six *U*s encapsulated by the twin *T* triplets. Note that the normal word order of the sentence has been modified in order to obtain this effect with its rather odd "*derzhit menia i tesnit*" 'confines me and constricts' rather than the more usual "confines and constricts me." Returning to the key word *tut*, we note that the two *T*s echo the twin *T*s of "*temnaia tiur'ma*," Cincinnatus's "dark dungeon." Moreover, they enclose and confine the "uuu" sound which is the Russian expression of fright or terror, as well as the initial vowel of *úzhas* 'terror', a word that is inserted in the midst of the alliterative *T*s of the above sentence and that, like *tut* itself, is purposefully scattered throughout the book.

These phonetic features are merely the beginning of the intricacies surrounding *tut*. In addition to being used as a lexical and auditory symbol of the wretched world it bespeaks, *tut* also is being employed as a visual icon. Let us take a final look at the sentence in question: "*Tupoe 'tut' podpertoe i zapertoe chetoiu 'tverdo,' temnaia tiur'ma, v kotoruiu zakliuchen neuemno voiushchii uzhas, derzhit menia i tesnit*" (98–99/93). The "*tverdo*" here is not the Russian adverb "firmly" (as many Russians assume it to be), but the homomorphic Old Church Slavonic name for the letter *T*. Again using the device of alphabetic iconicism, Nabokov is calling the Russian reader's attention to thematically relevant visual aspects of the important word *TuT*. Not only do its two *T*s echo the twin *T*s of *Temnaia Tiur'ma* 'dark dungeon,' but they visually resemble the two tall sentinels (*tiuremshchiki* 'jailers', if you will) towering over and confining the "*u*" of Cincinnatus's moan of terror.

This Russian tour de force presents severe difficulties in translation from the point of view of its phonetic and iconic properties. If the phonetic symbolism of the Russian *tut* (here) is to be retained in the English, the latter must provide a semantically equivalent sentence phonetically structured on the sounds of HERE, that is, "this world," just as the Russian original incorporates its improbable sequence of *T*s, *U*s, and *T*s so as to obtain the thematic key word *TTTUUUUUUTTT*. Strict adherence to this pattern is, of course, impossible, but Nabokov and his son, Dmitri, who is cited as the translator, make a prodigious if not entirely successful attempt: "Not

HERE! The HoRRiblE 'HERE,' the dark dungEon, in wHicH a RElEntlEssly Howling HEaRt is incaRcERatEd, this 'HERE' Holds and constricts mE." This manages to capture the necessary letters (HERE), but not in the eloquent pattern of the Russian with its triplets of *T*s symmetrically bracketing the prolonged exclamation of horror – UUUUUU. The *úzhas* 'horror', which auditorily and lex- ically embodies Cincinnatus's moan, is replaced by *heart*, which faintly echoes the sound of the key word *here* but loses the auditory mimicry of the Russian exclamation of horror. The latter effect is, however, picked up in the English text by the "ow" of "howling."[17] The visual, iconic aspect of the sentence is completely lost in transla- tion. Comparison of the English text with that of the Russian shows that Nabokov has simply omitted the phrase "*podpertoe i zapertoe chetoiu 'tverdo'*" (supported and locked in by its pair of *T*s) that sup- plied the Church Slavonic letter underlying the sentinel imagery described above.

In sum, Nabokov has managed to preserve much of the ingenious phonetic symbolism of the original but has been forced to forego completely the alphabetic iconicism which in the Russian original is consistently associated with the prison-house of language theme. It is unfortunate that this particular bit of alphabetic imagery had to be sacrificed for, as we have remarked above, the *tut* image, which is one pole of the major opposition underlying the book's theme, has been cunningly elaborated into a multileveled microcosm phonetically and visually (as well as lexically) expressive of the plight of Cincin- natus, the artist-prisoner.

As the day of Cincinnatus's beheading draws ever nearer, his fear that he will not succeed in conveying his vision mounts: "[A]h, I think I shall yet be able to express it all – the dreams, the coales- cence, the disintegration – no, again I am off the track – all my best words are deserters and do not answer the trumpet call, and the remainder are cripples" (205/200). He continues:

Oh, if only I had known that I was yet to remain here for such a long time, I would have begun *at the beginning* and gradually, along a highway of logically connected ideas, would have attained, would have completed, my soul would have surrounded itself with a structure of words. (205/200) [My emphasis – D.B.J.]

———

Akh, znai ia, chto tak dolgo eshche ostanus' tut, ia by *nachal s azov* i, postepenno, stolbovoi dorogoi sviaznykh poniatii, doshel by, dove-rshil by, dusha by obstroilas' slovami. (200) [My emphasis – D.B.J.]

In the English text Cincinnatus wishes to start his discovery process from "the beginning." This is the idea in the Russian text as well, but the latter entails a richer set of implications – both thematically and structurally. Instead of "at the beginning," the Russian text literally says "I would start from the *az*s." *Az* is the proper name of the first letter of the Old Church Slavonic alphabet. This usage of the Slavonic, although closely associated with the prison-house of language theme, is somewhat different in that no visual icon is involved. There is a significant bit of word play, however. In Church Slavonic, *az*, as well as being a letter name, is the first person singular pronoun "I," "ego." Thus Cincinnatus, in addition to using the cliché "to start from the beginning, from the letter A," is also saying that, given the opportunity, he would have delivered a revelation from his inner-most self for, as he observes, he is unique, the only person possessed of truth. In Russian usage, as in English, the initial and final alpha-betic letters are bound together in stock expressions such as *ot aza do izhitsy* 'from alpha to omega', that is, 'from beginning to end'. The expression presumably goes back to Revelation 1:8. "I am Alpha and Omega, the beginning and ending, saith the Lord, which is, and which was, and which is to come, the Almighty." Thus the utterance of Cincinnatus the artist, about starting from *az*, from the beginning, from his innermost self, has a certain theological resonance for the Russian reader.[18]

The alphabetic word play based on *az* is of interest in still another sense for while it is of itself less striking than the other examples, it occupies a position of marked symmetry in the use of the alphabetic device throughout the narrative. The novel is divided into twenty chapters, each of which (excepting the last two) covers one day of Cincinnatus's imprisonment. Cincinnatus is sentenced and arrives in his death cell in chapter 1; the beheading occurs in chapter 20. The first occurrence of the prison-house of language theme and its associated device of alphabetic iconicism is in chapter 2 and involves the letter *izhitsa*. The last occurrence of the theme and its alphabetic token is in chapter 19 and involves the letter *az*. The formal parallelism of the symmetrically placed chapters is marked in still other ways. The first sentence of chapter 2 is "The morning papers, brought to him with a cup of tepid chocolate by Rodion . . . teemed as always with color photographs" (23/35). The opening words of chapter 19 are "Next morning they brought him the newspapers, and this reminded him of the first days of his confinement. He noticed at once the color photograph" (202/197). Returning now to the alphabetic images, we note that the *izhitsa* that occurs in chapter 2 is the omega of the Church Slavonic alphabet, and the *az* of chapter 19 is the alpha. First, we may observe that the alphabet series from *az* to *izhitsa*, from alpha to omega, is, like Cincinnatus's life span, now complete. Second, we may ponder what significance, if any, lies in the curious fact that it is the omega letter *izhitsa* that is introduced first and the alpha letter *az* last, each in its carefully and symmetrically counterpoised chapters. It may, of course, be by chance, but chance plays a negligible role in Nabokov's work.

As we have remarked, the novel is structured along an axis of parallel oppositions of which the most basic is "this world" versus "that world," or "here" versus "there." This world, the world of Cincinnatus's imprisonment, is an evil monolith, a society of people whose very awareness is imprisoned by their hermetic language. In contrast, Cincinnatus visualizes a society opposite in every way to his own, its reversed mirror image, an ideal world. Borrowing terminology from another Nabokov work (*Ada*), we might call these worlds "Terra" and "Anti-Terra," where Cincinnatus finds himself, as he says, "through an error" (91/96). There are hints throughout the book that life on "Anti-Terra" is illusory, a dream state from which

Cincinnatus will awaken to find himself amid beings of his own kind on "Terra the Fair."[19] The moment of transition between these two worlds, the moment of awakening, is death. Taking this mirror image concept as an interpretive context, the placement of the omega before the alpha reveals its full significance. The number of days of Cincinnatus's life on "Anti-Terra" – devoted to his vain attempt to grasp and explicate "Terra the Fair" – is rapidly approaching zero, the moment of death: death from the point of view of "this world," but birth from the viewpoint of "that world," Cincinnatus's ideal world. Granted Cincinnatus's plight on Anti-Terra (*tut*), it is understandable and apt that the liturgical letters he uses in his vain struggle to penetrate and convey Terra (*tam*) are in reverse order. It is also apropos that he arrives at the beginning, *az* 'the I, the ego', on the day of his Anti-Terran death.

The final appearance of the prison-house of language theme with its alphabetic symbol occurs in the last entry in Cincinnatus's prison journal. As he continues the passage cited above, Cincinnatus is interrupted (just as he has written and crossed out the word *death*) by the unexpected arrival of Pierre who is to escort him to the place of the ceremony, the coup de grâce. As a condemned man Cincinnatus is offered a choice of last wishes. Rejecting those proffered, he asks for three minutes "'[t]o finish writing something' . . . but then he frowned, straining his thoughts, and suddenly understood that everything had in fact been written already" (209/204). Cincinnatus, the artist, has come to understand the truth of "this world," that he cannot escape the prison-house of language. Only after the axe falls and the world of "here" disintegrates can Cincinnatus make his way toward that other world in which "to judge by the voices, stood beings akin to him" (223/218), that is, beings who speak and understand his language.

The novel, like other Nabokov works, is about language and art, literature and the *littérateur*.[20] We have demonstrated at some length the theme of the prison-house of language – a theme that is a central concern of every serious writer. Cincinnatus is the paradigm of the writer; his plight, that of every verbal artist. The spartan furnishing of the novel, its almost schematic structuring, throw the theme and the intricate subpatterns of its exposition into high relief. Given that the language of art is simultaneously the theme of the novel and the means of expressing that theme, it is difficult to conceive a more apt motif than that of the alphabetic letters which are themselves the building blocks of the prison. The iconic letters, a device of indisputable ingenuity but necessarily of limited application, represent an attempt to loosen the fetters of the prison-house of language, for in their visual aspect they reach beyond the conventional lexical level of language toward a mystical ideal tongue in which words mime as well as mean, an artistic language of perfect clarity in which the correspondence between perception and percept and percept and word is absolute.

The alphabetic motif pervades the novel but, as we have noted, only one special manifestation of it is linked to the prison-house of language theme – the iconic use of Old Church Slavonic letters. Cincinnatus is striving to use language to break through the walls of this world and describe an ideal world. What could be more appropriate than the mysterious alphabetic tokens of an archaic religious tongue – a language intended solely to intimate to the prisoners of this world the truth and beauty of the next.[21]

Invitation to a Beheading is the most formalized and abstract of Nabokov's novels. Action is minimal and the characters, apart from Cincinnatus, are deliberately fashioned as cardboard figures whose costumes and makeup can be and often are changed and interchanged. It is the most overtly "modernist" and antirealistic of Nabokov' works. The book has been stripped of any human flesh (in character and event) in order to achieve maximal focus on a form and style that is of great technical brilliance and is distinctively appropriate to its theme.

NOTES

1. This essay is a condensed revision of a section from D. Barton Johnson, *Worlds in Regression: Some Novels of Vladimir Nabokov* (Ann Arbor, Mich.:

Ardis, 1985), 28–46. Another study in the same volume, "The Two Worlds of *Invitation to a Beheading*," 157–70, expands on the cosmological views set forth in the present essay.

2. *Speak, Memory* (New York: G. P. Putnam's Sons, 1966), 34–36; and *Drugie berega* (New York: Chekhov, 1954), 27–28.

3. Andrew Field, *Nabokov: His Life in Part* (New York: Little, Brown, 1977), 149.

4. For a detailed account of Nabokov's alphabetic chromesthesia and its role in his creative process, see D. Barton Johnson, *Worlds in Regression*, 10–27.

5. Nabokov interview with Lee Belser, *Los Angeles Evening Mirror News*, 31 July 1959.

6. It has been plausibly suggested by Brian Boyd and Alexander Dolinin that Nabokov's central plot idea for *Invitation to a Beheading* – a man in prison awaiting his fate – had its genesis in his then just completed biography of N. G. Chernyshevsky, the book within *The Gift*. Although mocking the radical martyr's political and aesthetic ideas, Nabokov was perhaps moved by Chernyshevsky's sad history. The parallels between Chernyshevsky and Cincinnatus are elaborated in Nora Buhks, "Eshafot v khrustal'nom dvortse: o romane Vl. Nabokova *Priglashenie na kazn'*," *Cahiers du Monde russe* 35.4 (1994): 821–38.

7. Beginning with Sergej Davydov's *"Teksty-Matreški" Vladimira Nabo-kova* (Munich: Otto Sagner, 1982), much has been written about detailed correspondences between various aspects of Gnosticism and *Invitation to a Beheading*. Although there seems to be some basis for such an approach, one should keep in mind that in Nabokov's Russian original Cincinnatus's crime was "gnoseologicheskaia gnusnost'," not "gnosticheskaia gnusnost'," that is, gnoseological turpitude, not "gnostical." "Gnoseology" is a synonym of "epistemology," whereas "Gnosticism" refers to a particular system of belief. Nabokov is not known to have read Gnostic source materials. It cannot be denied, however, that Nabokov endorsed the translation of "gnoseologicheskii" as "gnostic," but this may have been an afterthought, since the English translation was made some thirty years later. Also, the novel's emphasis on its characters as "specters, etc.," may owe quite as much to Gogol as to Gnosticism. See Nabokov's *Nikolai Gogol* (New York: New Directions, 1961). A more recent study of the novel's gnoseological/gnostic connections may be found in Caroline Schramm, "Gnosis und poetologische

Umkodierung: *Priglašenie na kazn'* von Vladimir Nabokov," Ph.D. diss., Universität Konstanz, 1994.

8. Page citations are to the following editions: Vladimir Nabokov, *Invitation to a Beheading*, trans. Dmitri Nabokov in collaboration with the author (New York: Capricorn, 1965); *Priglashenie na kazn'* (Paris: Editions Victor, 1960). Page numbers to the English and Russian texts are cited in the following format: (English page number / Russian page number).

9. The allusion is to the biblical Salome, her famous dance, and the head of John the Baptist. For a discussion of this, one of several beheading motifs, see Gavriel Shapiro, "The Salome Motif in Nabokov's *Invitation to a Beheading*," *Nabokov Studies* 3 (1996). Shapiro also discusses a number of the novel's allusions to Russian literature in "Russkie literaturnye alliuzii v romane Nabokova *Priglashenie na kazn'*," *Russian Literature* 9.4 (1981): 369–78; and in "Khristianskie motivy, ikh ikonografiia i simvolika, v romane Vladimira Nabokova *Priglashenie na kazn'*," *Russian Language Journal* 33, no. 116 (1979): 144–62. See also Pekka Tammi, "Invitation to a Decoding. Dostoevskij as Subtext in Nabokov's *Priglašenie na kazn'*," *Scando-Slavica* 32 (1986): 51–72. Gennady Barabtarlo addresses two of the novel's principal motifs in "Within and Without Cincinnatus's Cell: Reference Gauges in Nabokov's *Invitation to a Beheading*," *Slavic Review* 49.3 (1990): 390–97. See also Guy Houk, "The Spider and the Moth: Nabokov's *Priglašenie na kazn'* as Epistemological Exhortation," *Russian Literature* 18 (1985): 31–41.

10. The word *fita* originally designated the Church Slavonic letter Θ (the Greek letter theta), which was replaced by Φ after the orthographical reforms of 1917.

11. I owe this expression to Frederic Jameson's *The Prison-House of Language. A Critical Account of Structuralism and Russian Formalism* (Princeton, N.J.: Princeton University Press, 1972). Jameson in turn has borrowed it from Nietzsche whom he quotes in his epigraph: "We have to cease to think if we refuse to do it in the prison-house of language; for we cannot reach further than the doubt which asks whether the limit we see is really a limit." Nabokov's novel can be viewed as an exploration of this statement.

12. Nabokov's "Englishing" of the Russian word *prashcha* as *catapult* is presumably a throwback to his Anglo-Russian childhood. *Catapult* is the usual British term for the American "slingshot."

13. This sentence is emphasized in the English but not the Russian text.

14. For a discussion of another aspect of this theme, see Brian Thomas

Oles, "Silence and the Ineffable in Nabokov's *Invitation to a Beheading*," *Nabokov Studies* 2 (1995): 191–212.

15. While Cincinnatus's attempt to express his vision by writing is a major theme, Cincinnatus and the reader are equally engaged in a creative reading process. This aspect is explored in Stephen Blackwell, "Reading and Rupture in Nabokov's *Invitation to a Beheading*," *Slavic and East European Journal* 39.1 (1994): 38–53.

16. The English text differs from the Russian in several ways. The initial solitary *tam* of the Russian is expanded into the trilingual triplet "*There, tam, là-bas*" in the English, while the numerous subsequent occurrences of "there" are italicized. The contrasting *tut* of the Russian has been expanded to "in this world." As we have shown and shall show, the exigencies of translation have resulted in the loss of some of Nabokov's alphabetic icons and weakened, in still other ways, the force of the *tut/tam* opposition so central to the novel. Many of the differences between the two texts have to do with Nabokov's effort to retain the opposition. See also Robert Hughes, "Notes on the Translation of *Invitation to a Beheading*" in *Nabokov: Criticism, Reminiscences, Translations and Tributes*, ed. Alfred Appel, Jr., and Charles Newman (Evanston, Ill.: Northwestern University Press, 1971), 284–92.

17. Nabokov's revisions of the draft English translation suggest that he attempted to augment the number of *Hs*, *Rs* and *Es* so as to parallel the anagrammatic Russian *Ts* and *U*. The typescript of Dmitri Nabokov's English translation with his father's handwritten alterations is in container number 3 of the Vladimir Nabokov Papers held at the Manuscript Division of the Library of Congress, as is Nabokov's original Russian manuscript. The passage in question is on page 141 of the translation typescript.

18. This resonance is reinforced by another pointed use of an Old Church Slavonicism elsewhere in the book. In his prison journal Cincinnatus speaks of his gradual reduction to an irreducible nucleus that says "*Ia esm*'" 'I am' (95/96). The use of *esm*' here is purely Church Slavonic.

19. See, for example, 92/97 and 209/213, as well as the novel's concluding paragraph.

20. The earliest and most eloquent statement of this assertion was made by the émigré poet and critic Vladislav Khodasevich in his 1937 essay "O Sirine" (On Sirin), *Izbrannaia proza*, ed. Nina Berberova (New York: Russica, 1982). A partial translation may be found in Appel and Newman, *Nabokov: Criticism*, 96–101.

21. The use of the equivalent Greek letters to convey some of the alphabetic icons in the English translation fails to capture an important dimension of the original. The Old Church Slavonic letters are firmly and exclusively associated in the minds of all Russians (at least those of Nabokov's generation) with the ecclesiastic language and its implications of spiritual transcendence. Although the New Testament was written in Greek, the Greek letters have no such resonance for speakers of English.

III  PRIMARY SOURCES

"Welcome to the Block": Priglashenie na kazn' / Invitation to a Beheading, A Documentary Record

BRIAN BOYD

The following selection of documents, mostly unpublished, records, as much as archives can, the story of *Invitation to a Beheading* during Nabokov's lifetime. The only major omission is the readily available text of his 1959 foreword to the novel's first translation into English.

Since this is the first time such documentation has been assembled for any of his works, it will allow readers to see the kinds of materials available in a representative cross-section of Nabokov's archives and the contrast between the relative paucity of information for his years of European exile and the fullness of the record for his later years.

Nabokov never knew of and could hardly have envisaged the celebrated 1989 Moscow staging of *Invitation to a Beheading*, but his archives already reveal that more than any other of his works, *Invitation to a Beheading* has inspired other artists – especially dramatists – to adapt it for their chosen medium.

The final two entries in this selection are aptly poignant: a reference to the Czech edition, for which Nabokov had granted the rights but which was abruptly quashed by the Soviet invasion of 1968, and Véra Nabokov's comment, two years after her husband's death, that it made no sense to call the novel a work of despair, since the ending was more optimistic than not.

Origins are always mysterious, as Nabokov stressed especially in *The Gift*, although it is precisely in that novel that we must look for the origin of *Invitation to a Beheading* – unless we delve deeper into the past: to 1930, when Nabokov had several meetings with Dietrich, a German student he "wanted to file for possible use,"[1] whose "hobby was capital punishment, and who saw it done with an axe in Regensburg," and informed him that "the headsman was positively paternal"[2]; to 1923, when he had written a play, *Dedushka* (*The Grand-dad*), that shows a man who has climbed the scaffold to his death but is still alive twenty-five years later; to 1922, when his own father was assassinated just after writing a last article that happened to put the case against capital punishment[3]; to 1906, when his father, as parliamentary leader of the Constitutional Democrats, introduced into the First State Duma a bill outlawing capital punishment; to 1881, when, as Minister of Justice, Nabokov's grandfather, anxious to end the spectacles that he thought public executions had become, ordered that henceforth they would be carried out within prison walls in the presence only of officials and public witnesses; to 1864, when the writer Nikolay Chernyshevsky had to face a ritual mock-execution before receiving his actual sentence of exile; to 1849, when Dostoevsky and his fellow Petrashevtsy had to undergo what they were convinced would be a real execution before learning that their sentences had been commuted to exile; to the Decembrist Rebellion of 1825 and the hanging of poet Kondraty Ryleev – on whose estate and its *chemin du pendu* Nabokov would play so often as a child – and the haunting possibility that had Pushkin not been more cautious than his Decembrist friends, his supreme imagination too might have been cut off on the scaffold.

If the theme of execution runs through Nabokov's and Russia's past, it was not until after he began *Dar* (*The Gift*) that something unexpectedly jolted him into writing a whole novel on the subject. Starting work on *Dar* early in 1933, he first focused on the two sections that needed thorough research, Fyodor's father's expeditions to Central Asia and Fyodor's iconoclastic *Life of Chernyshevsky*. By the spring of 1934 he was deep in the Chernyshevsky biography, as a letter of April 26, 1934, to Vladislav Khodasevich makes clear,[4] but something caused him to set *Dar* aside to work intensely on a new novel, *Priglashenie na kazn'*, between June 24 and September 15, 1934. Although he later remembered the period of its composition as "one fortnight of wonderful excitement and sustained inspiration,"[5] this seems a subjective condensation of the nearly four months separating the first and last dates on the manuscript – still an extraordinarily rapid burst of composition for a complex novel – unless perhaps the "September 15" date records the end of a subsequent draft. Late in December 1934 he was still making final adjustments to the typescript which he had dictated to his wife Véra.

Already some time before that he had evidently broached with Vadim Rudnev the possibility of sending an excerpt from the life of Chernyshevsky to *Sovremennye zapiski*, which suggests that although he may have later revised this chapter (in a letter to his New York agent, Altagracia de Janelli, he writes that the Chernyshevsky chapter "took *me* four years to write"),[6] he had thought it already fit for publication before he suddenly broke off to write *Priglashenie na kazn'*. Even if we do not know exactly when he finalized the phrasing of the first passage below (from chapter 3, describing the process of Fyodor's composing his life of Chernyshevsky), the content of these lines seems unmistakeably to have caused him to swerve aside from *Dar*, the last hundred years, and realism, and toward *Priglashenie na kazn'*, the future, and fantasy.[7]

If that makes the two novels sound polar opposites, in a sense they are. But they are also companions. In *Dar* Nabokov had found a new way to meld prose and poetry, in the verse that takes form as rhymed stanzas in Fyodor's mind but that he prints as prose when he recounts his own past. And *Priglashenie na kazn'*, Nabokov maintained, was the only prose poem he ever composed.[8]

FROM CHAPTER 3 OF *DAR* / *THE GIFT*. WRITTEN 1934 (–1937?)

He sincerely admired the way Chernyshevski, an enemy of capital punishment, made deadly fun of the poet Zhukovski's infamously benign and meanly sublime proposal to surround executions with a mystic secrecy (since, in public, he said, the condemned man brazenly puts on a bold face, thus bringing the law into disrepute) so that those attending the hanging would not see but would only hear solemn church hymns from behind a curtain, for an execution should be moving. And while reading this Fyodor recalled his father saying that innate in every man is the feeling of something insuperably abnormal about the death penalty, something like the uncanny reversal of action in a looking glass that makes everyone left-handed: not for nothing is everything reversed for the executioner: the horse-collar is put on upside down when the robber Razin is taken to the scaffold; wine is poured for the headsman not with a natural turn of the wrist but backhandedly; and if, according to the Swabian code, an insulted actor was permitted to seek satisfaction by striking the *shadow* of the offender, in China it was precisely an actor – a shadow – who fulfilled the duties of the executioner, all responsibility being as it were lifted from the world of men into the inside-out one of mirrors.

The Gift,[9] 215

MANUSCRIPT OF *PRIGLASHENIE NA KAZN'*

[213 pp., heavily revised, dated at the beginning (p. 1) "24•VI•34"[10] and at the end (p. "208"), "15•IX•34"]
Library of Congress Nabokov Archive (LCNA), Box 3, folder 1

FROM VN LETTER TO ELENA IVANOVNA NABOKOV,[11] SEPTEMBER 14, 1934

Нынче кончаю роман, а переписка на машинке займет месяц.

Today I'm finishing a novel, but typing it out will take a month.
Vladimir Nabokov Archive (VNA)

FROM VN LETTER TO ZINAIDA SHAKHOVSKOY,[12]
SEPTEMBER 15, 1934

У меня был грип, не мог повернуть голову, --вот причина того,
что не сразу ответил. [. . .]
Я только-что кончил новый роман: "Приглашение на казнь."

I had the flu, couldn't turn my head, – that's why I didn't answer
straight away. [. . .]
I've just finished a new novel: "Invitation to a Beheading."
Shakhovskoy Collection, Library of Congress

FROM VN LETTER TO VADIM RUDNEV,[13]
NOVEMBER 25, 1934

Простите, что только теперь пишу, -- в последнее время денно
ношно диктовал в машинку новый роман "Приглашение на казнь."
Еще дней десять провожусь, сверяя, а затем пришлю Вам
экземпляр.

Sorry to be writing only now – lately I have been dictating my
new novel *Invitation to a Beheading* into the typewriter day and night.
I'll take about another ten days checking, and then will send you a
copy.
Vadim Rudnev Papers, University of Illinois,
Urbana-Champaign[14]

FROM VN LETTER TO ELENA NABOKOV,
DECEMBER 6, 1934

Я более или менее кончил возню с романом, и ты его скоро получишь.

I have more or less finished fussing over the novel, and you'll get it soon.

VNA

FROM VN LETTER TO VADIM RUDNEV,
DECEMBER 27, 1934

На-днях получите наконец манускрипт: только теперь кончаю исправления и проверку. Анна Лазаревна Вам говорила о моем материальном положении. Благодарю Вас за предложение аванса, он мне был бы очень кстати. А.Л. мне сказала, что в ближайшем номере С.З. мог бы появиться что-нибудь маленькое из моих вещей, она в разговоре с Вами упомянула об отрывке из Чернышевского. Я и сам думал что-либо оттуда урвать, но рассмотрев написанное, пришел к заключению, что ни из Чернышевского, ни из того романа, которого он будет одним из элементов, извлечь пока ничего нельзя, не повредив целого.

In a few days you will at last receive the manuscript: only now am I finishing the corrections and checking. Anna Lazarevna[15] has told you about my material situation. Thanks for the offer of an advance, it would be very handy. A. L. told me a little something of mine could appear in the next issue of *S.Z.*; she reminded you during your chat about an excerpt from the Chernyshevsky. I myself had thought of plucking something from there, but after looking over what I've written, I have come to the conclusion that for the moment I can't excerpt anything from the Chernyshevsky, nor from the novel of which it will form part, without harming the whole.

VNA

FROM VN LETTER TO VADIM RUDNEV,
FEBRUARY 11, 1935

Относительно "Приглашения на казнь" принимаю все Ваши соображения. Ни на какие сокращения конечно согласиться не могу. Над романом "о Чернышевском" работаю уже два года, но он совершенно не готов для печати, не говоря уж о том, что круг читателей, которым он будет доступен, будет пожалуй еще ограниченее.

With regard to "Invitation to a Beheading" I accept all your points. Of course I can't agree to any cuts. On the Chernyshevsky novel I have been working for two years now; it's quite unready for print, to say nothing of the fact that the circle of readers to whom it will be accessible will be perhaps even more limited.

VNA

FROM VN LETTER TO ELENA IVANOVNA NABOKOV,
MARCH 10, 1935

I'm afraid твое толкование "Приглашения" совершенно неверно. Никакого не следует искать символа или иносказания. Он строго логичен и реален; он -- самая простая ежедневная действительность, никаких особых объяснений не требующая.

I'm afraid your explanation of "Invitation" is completely wrong. You don't have to look for symbols or allegory. It's strictly logical and real; it's the simplest everyday reality, it doesn't require any special explanation.

VNA

FROM LETTER TO ELENA IVANOVNA NABOKOV,
APRIL 27, 1935

Только-что отослал "Совр. Зап." корректуру "Приглашения."

I've just sent "Sovr. Zap." the proofs of "Invitation."

VNA

SOVREMENNYE ZAPISKI, 58, JUNE 27, 1935[16]

[First publication of *Priglashenie na kazn'*, chapters 1–6]

SOVREMENNYE ZAPISKI, 59, NOVEMBER 19, 1935[17]

[First publication of *Priglashenie na kazn'*, chapters 7–13]

SOVREMENNYE ZAPISKI, 60, FEBRUARY 28, 1936[18]

[First publication of *Priglashenie na kazn'*, chapters 14–20]

ON LETTER FROM KARIN DE LAVAL[19] TO VN,
JANUARY 18, 1937, IN VÉRA NABOKOV'S HAND

отвечено 23.1.37
[...]
3) Пригл. на казнь. Петрополис вероятно скоро за него возьмется, т.к. заканчивает юбилейное издание Пушкина, задержавшее остальные книги.

answered 23.1.37
[...]
3). Inv. to Beheading. Petropolis[20] will probably start it soon, since it's finishing the Jubilee edition of Pushkin, which has been holding up the rest of its books.

LCNA, Box 8, folder 14

FROM VN LETTER TO ILIA ISIDOROVICH FONDAMINSKY,[21]
AUGUST 16, 1937

Меня еще очень волнует вопрос "Приглашения на казнь."

The question of "Invitation to a Beheading" still worries me greatly.[22]

LCNA, Box 8, folder 14

FROM LETTER FROM VLADIMIR ZENZINOV[23] TO VN,
SEPTEMBER 3, 1937

Я смогу ее взять не раньше конца года.

I can't take it earlier than the end of the year.

LCNA, Box 8, folder 14

FROM VN LETTER TO ALTAGRACIA DE JANNELLI,[24]
MAY 18, 1938

I am afraid I shall always remain "objective" and that I shall never, never, never write novels solving "modern problems" or picturing "the world unrest." I am neither Upton Sinclair nor Sinclair Lewis. Literature will always remain a game for me, the secret rules of which preclude my following any aim foreign to its curiously divine nature. Incidentally I don't see much difference between Sov. Russia and Germany: it is the same kind of boot with the nails somewhat bloodier in the former one. On the other hand in my novels "Invit." and my last one the "Gift" I have in my own way reflected things and moods which are in direct connection with the times we live in. I am sorry there is no translation of these two books (one a fantasy, the other a full power novel of 500 pages) as either of them – and especially the second – ought to be published in America. [25]

VNA

FROM VN LETTER TO ZINAIDA SHAKHOVSKOY,
C. SEPTEMBER 1938

Французское "Отчаяние" (Ла Меприз) еще не вышло, а "Приглашение на казнь" только-что откорректировали.

The French "Despair" (La Méprise) is still not out, but they have just done the corrected proofs of "Invitation to a Beheading."

Shakhovskoy Collection, Library of Congress

POSLEDNIE NOVOSTI,[26] NOVEMBER 24, 1938

[Priglashenie na kazn' listed among Knigi dlia otzyva (Books for review)]

VOZROZHDENIE,[27] FEBRUARY 17, 1939

[Priglashenie na kazn' on sale for $1]

FROM VN LETTER TO ZINAIDA SHAKHOVSKOY, MARCH 29, 1939

2го апреля еду в Лондон, где 5го читаю у Сабл. Считаешь-ли ты ладной мыслью заехать мне на обратном пути в Брюссель, чтобы там дать вечер -- русский, или два, русский и французский (т.е. я бы мог читать главы из перевода "Пригл. на казнь" только-что законченного замечательным переводчиком Jarl Priel).

On April 2 I go to London, where on the fifth I read at Sabl.[28] Do you think it a good idea for me to call in on the return journey to Brussels, to arrange an evening there – a Russian one, or two, a Russian and a French (i.e., I could read a chapter of the translation of "Inv. to a Beheading" just finished by a wonderful translator, Jarl Priel).

Shakhovskoy Collection, Library of Congress

FROM VN LETTER TO EDMUND WILSON,[29]
DECEMBER 15, 1940

[On Wilson's picture of Lenin in his *To the Finland Station*]
That bluff geniality, that screwing up of eyes (*s prishchurinkoy*),
that boyish laugh, etc., on which his biographers dwell so lovingly,
form something particularly distasteful to me. It is this atmosphere
of joviality, this pail of milk of human kindness with a dead rat at the
bottom, that I have used in my *Invitation to a Beheading* (which I still
hope you will read). The "invitation" is so kindly meant, all will be so
nice and pleasant, if only you don't make a fuss (says the executioner
to his "patient"). A German friend of mine, whose hobby was capital
punishment, and who saw it done with an axe in Regensburg, told
me that the headsman was positively paternal.

Nabokov-Wilson Letters (*NWL*), 33

FROM VN LETTER TO JAMES LAUGHLIN,[30]
NOVEMBER 27, 1941

The translation of *Invitation to a Beheading* is progressing at a very
slow pace.

VNA

FROM VN LETTER TO EDMUND WILSON,
JANUARY 5, 1942

I am writing a new novel in English; but moreover there are at
least three Russian novels of mine which I would like to have translated and published. I wrote to Laughlin telling him that several
publishers have approached me and that if he did not want those
three Russian novels I might try and offer them elsewhere keeping
for him the English novel I am writing now. I also told him that I
could not find the right kind of translator (the first chapters of
Invitation to a Beheading which one of my translators has just sent me
are one long shudder).

NWL, 55

FROM VN LETTER TO JARL PRIEL, MARCH 17, 1946

[asks Priel if he can find his 1939 translation into French of *Priglashenie na kazn'*]

VNA

FROM JARL PRIEL LETTER TO VN, MARCH 23, 1946

[has been able to find only part of] mon brouillon (mais avec vos corrections) . . . vos précieuses corrections

[. . .] my draft (but with your corrections) . . . your precious corrections

VNA

"EXILE," WRITTEN FEBRUARY–APRIL 1950[31]

But the author that interested me most was naturally Sirin. . . . His first two novels are to my taste mediocre; among the other six or seven the most haunting are *Invitation to a Beheading*, which deals with the incarceration of a rebel in a picture-postcard fortress by the buffoons and bullies of a Communazist state; and *Luzhin's Defense*, . . .

Conclusive Evidence, 216–17

FROM DOUSSIA ERGAZ[32] LETTER TO VN,
DECEMBER 24, 1952

[A translator will do a sample translation from *Priglashenie na kazn'*, since no French publisher will take Priel's version, which is no doubt] fidèle, mais horriblement lourde quant au français.

[. . .] faithful, but horribly heavy in its French.

VNA

FROM VN LETTER TO DOUSSIA ERGAZ,
DECEMBER 29, 1952

INVITATION AU SUPPLICE. Je regrette profondément que la merveilleuse traduction de Jarl Priel ne soit pas acceptée. Mais même si une nouvelle traduction de ce livre était à faire, le nouveau traducteur serait forcé à se baser sur celle de Jarl Priel que j'ai revue et corrigée à grande perte de temps il y a une quinzaine d'années. Il y a des passages dans ce livre – il y en a même beaucoup – qu'aucun traducteur ne pourrait tourner de la manière que je désire. Je me suis appliqué à traduire ces passages, et Priel les a incorporés dans sa traduction. Il ne me serait pas possible de recommencer ce labeur. Et il y a aussi le titre – une trouvaille de Jarl Priel – dont il faudra se servir. Il n'y aurait donc rien à faire que de payer à Priel quelque chose pour la droit de se servir de sa traduction comme base. On pourrait ensuite chercher à en alleger et à en modifier le style jusqu'à ce que l'éditeur se trouve satisfait.

INVITATION AU SUPPLICE. I am very sorry that Jarl Priel's marvelous translation has not been approved. But even if a new translation has to be made, the new translator would be forced to base himself on Priel's, which I have looked over and corrected at a considerable cost in time fifteen years ago. There are passages in this book – many, even – that no translator could render in the way I want. I set myself to translate these passages, and Priel incorporated them in his translation. It would not be possible for me to start the task all over again. And there's also the title – Priel's find – which must be used. So there would be no choice but to pay Priel something for the right to use his translation as a base. We could then look to lighten and modify its style until the publisher felt satisfied.

VNA

FROM VN LETTER TO LÉON MARCANTONATOS,[33]
MARCH 14, 1953

Votre superbe traduction m'a fait un très vif et rare plaisir. Je ne saurais vous décrire les tourments que j'éprouve trop souvent, hélas, à la lecture de certaines traductions de mes livres, faites par des personnes qui jouissent pourtant d'une excellente réputation littéraire.

Je n'ai pas mon texte russe avec moi, mais ma femme vient de me lire votre traduction qui m'a semblé de toute beauté, avec toutes les nuances que j'avais cherché à rendre.

Your superb translation gave me great and rare pleasure. I couldn't tell you the torments I experience too often, alas, in reading certain translations of my books, done by people who nevertheless enjoy an excellent literary reputation.

I don't have my Russian text with me, but my wife has just read me your translation which seemed to me perfectly beautiful, with all the nuances I have tried to capture.

[Explains about the Priel translation]

VNA

FROM VÉRA NABOKOV LETTER TO ZINAIDA
SHAKHOVSKOY, AUGUST 5, 1954

Он очень взволновался, прочитав то, что ты пишешь о "Приглашении." Не помнишь ли, о каком переводе шла речь? Существует перевод (одобренный автором, но почему-то презираемый Mme Ergaz, который лет 15 назад сделал Jarl Priel). Существует перевод (кажется, частичный), который года два назад сделал греческий консул в Тунисе. Этот перевод великолепен. Но ходит где-то еще один--прескверный--перевод, а это В. беспокоит. Книга куплена на "Table Ronde," вместе с четырьмя другими, через Ergaz.

He's very worried after reading what you write about "Invitation." You don't remember which translation they were talking about? A translation exists (approved by the author, but for some reason despised by Mme Ergaz, done 15 years ago by Jarl Priel). A translation exists (incomplete, apparently), done two years ago by the Greek consul in Tunis. This translation is magnificent. But somewhere there's another – wretched – one going around, and this alarms V. The book was bought for "Table Ronde," together with four others, through Ergaz.

Shakhovskoy Collection, Library of Congress

FROM VÉRA NABOKOV LETTER TO DOUSSIA ERGAZ, NOVEMBER 15, 1956

The MS of the "Invitation" in translation has arrived safely. Many thanks.

VNA

FROM VÉRA NABOKOV LETTER TO DOUSSIA ERGAZ, MARCH 17, 1957

Mon mari [. . .] s'intéresse surtout à voir publier un de ses meilleurs livres aussitôt que possible,[34] et plus que tout il voudrait qu'un bon éditeur sorte INVITATION dans la traduction de Jarl Priel.

Above all my husband [. . .] is interested in seeing one of his best books published as soon as possible, and more than anything else he would like a good publisher to get INVITATION out in the Jarl Priel translation.

VNA

FROM VN LETTER TO DOUSSIA ERGAZ, MARCH 24, 1957

The translation by Jarl Priel is so endlessly superior to the work of, say, Mme Sibon;[35] moreover it has been revised by me and is ready for publication. Therefore, the best solution, to my mind, would be to publish it as is, without losing any more time in search of someone who would deliver – in a couple of years maybe – a new translation which I would have to revise from A to Z. I am convinced that it is important to get INVITATION into print without further delay.

VNA

FROM VN LETTER TO MICHEL MOHRT,[36] APRIL 12, 1958

[I am upset to hear they don't like the Priel translation] car elle me paraît excellente, que j'y ai travaillé avec lui et que, à mon avis, si elle manque peut-être de ce qu'on appelle en Amérique "smoothness" elle en gagne par sa fidelité et honnêteté.

———

[. . .] because it seems excellent to me, because I've worked with him and because to me, if it lacks a little what Americans call "smoothness" it makes up for it by its fidelity and honesty.[37]

VNA

FROM LETTER FROM DOUSSIA ERGAZ TO VN,
JULY 16, 1958

[Gallimard has at last agreed to publish INVITATION AU SUPPLICE]

VNA

FROM VN LETTER TO WALTER MINTON,[38]
AUGUST 29, 1958

I am writing you separately about INVITATION TO A BEHEADING. Two things the translator must be: 1) male, 2)

American-born or English. He must also have a sound and scholarly knowledge of Russian. I do not know of anyone who would meet these requirements except my son – but he is unfortunately much too busy and has already had to refuse to translate a book for Doubleday.

VNA

FROM VN LETTER TO MINTON, SEPTEMBER 8, 1958

[. . .] would you be so very kind and have the Russian copy of INVITATION TO A BEHEADING which I mailed to you, sent to my son.

VNA

FROM VN LETTER TO DAVID C. MEARNS,[39] DECEMBER 10, 1958

Tomorrow I shall ship to you by Railway Express a box of manuscripts, some Russian, some English; I am enclosing a list with this letter.
[. . .]
PRIGLASHENIE NA KAZN' (*Invitation to a Beheading*), MS, compl., 208 pp., ink, mostly on both sides of sheets. Publ. 1938, Dom Knigi, Paris, France. First serialized in *Sovr. Zap.*, Paris.

Library of Congress, Nabokov Correspondence File

FROM VN LETTER TO WALTER MINTON, JANUARY 8, 1959[40]

Dmitri showed me the beginning of his translation when he came here for Christmas. It is excellent but the pace is slow. He promised to try and develop more mph from now on.

VNA

FROM VN LETTER TO MINTON, JANUARY 12, 1959

I have talked to Dmitri again. The sample of translation he showed me is so good that I want him to drop his job with the "Digest of the Soviet Press" and work full-time on the translation of my books. Before I tell him this I would like to know what terms you would offer him for INVITATION TO A BEHEADING. Would you want to sign with me, too, an agreement now? The important thing, however, is to settle things with Dmitri about the translation.

VNA

FROM VN LETTER TO GEORGE WEIDENFELD,[41] JANUARY 12, 1959

[recommends that after *Lolita* Weidenfeld and Nicolson publish *Bend Sinister*, then *The Real Life of Sebastian Knight*, *Nabokov's Dozen*, and *Speak, Memory*]

After that I would have for you an English translation of my three best Russian novels: LUZHIN'S DEFENCE (the story of a demented chess player), THE GIFT (a novel of love and literature) and INVITATION TO A BEHEADING (a grim fantasy which at this moment is being translated into English by my son Dmitri for Putnam).

Selected Letters,[42] 273

FROM VN LETTER TO WALTER MINTON, JANUARY 20, 1959[43]

Something which has been bothering me. The title I originally suggested for PRIGLASHENIE NA KAZN' (INVITATION TO A BEHEADING) can be improved upon by the shorter: WELCOME TO THE BLOCK with its splendidly gruesome double entendre. The very good French translation which Gallimard has purchased is entitled INVITATION AU SUPPLICE.

VNA

FROM VN LETTER TO WALTER MINTON, MAY 18, 1959

I have not yet tackled the Fawcett proofs[44] and shall tell them it will take some time. Anyway, I intend first of all to attend to Dmitri's INVITATION. I talked to him yesterday from a glass booth in the wilderness[45] and asked him to send me the remaining part at once.

VNA

FROM VN LETTER TO WALTER MINTON, MAY 30, 1959

I have now in my hands more than three quarters of INVITA-TION in Dmitri's translation and am starting to check it next week.

VNA

DRAFT TYPESCRIPT OF *INVITATION TO A BEHEADING*

[TS of translation by Dmitri Nabokov, 365 pp., with VN's penciled corrections and changes]

LCNA, Box 3, folder 2

FROM VÉRA NABOKOV LETTER TO WALTER MINTON, JUNE 11, 1959

V. asks me to tell you that Dmitri's translation is superb, leaving so little to be changed that the typescript should be in your hands before July 1.

VNA

FOREWORD TO *INVITATION TO A BEHEADING*, WRITTEN JUNE 25, 1959

[MS, 4 pp., heavily corrected]

LCNA, Box 3, folder 2

FAIR-COPY TYPESCRIPT OF *INVITATION TO A BEHEADING*

[TS, setting copy, [8] + 233 pp. Holograph corrections in VN's hand]

LCNA, Box 3, folder 3

FROM VN LETTER TO WALTER MINTON, JUNE 29, 1959

I have great pleasure in sending you my INVITATION. You will notice that I have prefixed a rather racy foreword to it. I want to repeat that Dmitri did a magnificent job.

VNA

FROM VN LETTER TO WALTER MINTON, JULY 14, 1959

[. . .] the colloquial vulgarisms of the automatons of the book are integral features which must be rendered by corresponding vulgarisms in American English.

VNA

FROM VÉRA NABOKOV LETTER TO WALTER MINTON, JULY 29, 1959

Vladimir thanks you for the proofs of INVITATION. He is working on them and says that you will have them back within a few days.

VNA

FROM VN LETTER TO WALTER MINTON, AUGUST 4, 1959

I am returning today, separately, the corrected galleys of Invit. to a Behead.

VNA

PROOFS OF *INVITATION TO A BEHEADING*

[Galley proofs, corrected.]

LCNA, Box 3, folder 4

FROM VÉRA NABOKOV LETTER TO WALTER MINTON,
AUGUST 12, 1959

Dear Walter, Vladimir says:
Forget your worries: the text is just as it should be and corresponds exactly to the original. All three characters – Roman, Rodrig and Rodion – are facets of the same manyfaced monster.

VNA

INVITATION TO A BEHEADING

[First English-language (Putnam's Sons) edition published September 21, 1959]

FROM VN LETTER TO JARL PRIEL, NOVEMBER 23, 1959

votre belle traduction de mon roman "Invitation au Supplice" va enfin paraître dans quelques mois chez Gallimard. Pour des raisons que j'ignore on avait d'abord voulu en commander une nouvelle traduction, mais comme j'insistai sur la vôtre, on y a consenti, et maintenant on la trouve très belle.

your fine translation of my novel "Invitation to a Beheading" is at last going to appear from Gallimard in a few months. For reasons unknown to me they at first wanted to order a new translation, but as I insisted on yours, they agreed, and now they find it very good.

VNA

FROM WALTER MINTON LETTER TO VN AND VÉRA
NABOKOV, NOVEMBER 24, 1959

I wish I could report that INVITATION was selling well, but as
Vladimir said in his introduction, I am afraid we shall have to be
content with the few rather than the many.

VNA

FROM VÉRA NABOKOV LETTER TO WALTER MINTON,
DECEMBER 19, 1959

My husband has just received the beautifully bound copy of IN-
VITATION TO A BEHEADING.

VNA

FROM DOUSSIA ERGAZ LETTER TO VÉRA NABOKOV,
MARCH 24, 1960

[Despite repeated instructions about INVITATION AU SUP-
PLICE, Gallimard has passed beyond the first proof stage without
sending proofs to VN]

VNA

FROM VÉRA NABOKOV LETTER TO DOUSSIA ERGAZ,
MARCH 29, 1960

[There is nothing to be done about INVITATION AU SUP-
PLICE, although VN has not read it for twenty-two years] et croit
qu'il aurait pu apporter des corrections importantes aujourd'hui –
malgré le fait qu'il ait de l'admiration pour le style et le vocabulaire
de M. Priel.

[. . .] and thinks that he could now make important corrections –
despite his admiration for M. Priel's style and vocabulary.

VNA

FROM VÉRA NABOKOV LETTER TO MICHEL MOHRT,
APRIL 9, 1960

My husband was very much upset to find that the book (INVITA-TION AU SUPPLICE) went into production without his having seen the proofs. He asks me to remind you that he asked several times to be shown the proofs (my letters of Jan. 12 and Jan. 27), and that in your letter of Jan. 27 you wrote: "Enfin je n'oublie pas que je dois vous montrer les épreuves de 'L'INVITATION AU SUP-PLICE' dès que le texte aura été composé et vu une première fois par Monsieur Jarl Priel." Nous comprenons bien qu'il n'y a plus rien à faire à présent pour le premier tirage. Nous attendons donc les épreuves corrigées, ou un exemplaire du livre, pour que mon mari puisse faire des changements, si besoin il y a, pour le second tirage. Ce qui l'inquiète surtout c'est la petite preface qu'il n'a pas vu en traduction.

[...] "Finally I have not forgotten that I must show you the proofs of 'INVITATION AU SUPPLICE' as soon as the text has been typeset and Monsieur Jarl Priel has had a first look over it." We are quite aware that there's nothing more that can be done now for the first printing. We are therefore waiting for the corrected proofs, or a copy of the book, so that my husband can make any changes necessary for the second printing. What particularly worries him is the little preface which he hasn't seen in translation.

VNA

FROM VN LETTER TO WEIDENFELD AND NICOLSON,
APRIL 19, 1960

Must insist you delete in blurb all reference to Kafka and Orwell.

VNA

FROM VÉRA NABOKOV LETTER TO MICHEL MOHRT, APRIL 27, 1960

[VN is not happy with the translation of the preface, which he would like to delete altogether,] especially since in his opinion it does not have much interest for the French reader, being meant in the main for the English translation of the Russian text.

VNA

FROM VÉRA NABOKOV LETTER TO FRANK HARPER,[46] APRIL 28, 1960

My husband asks me to answer your letter of April 20. He is entirely and unequivocally opposed to capital punishment. He wishes you success in your fight against it. He regrets that he cannot write an article for you or sign a petition [for two reasons] – the first, because he thinks he has done his bit by writing a whole book on the subject ("Invitation to a Beheading"), and the second, because he never puts his signature for something he has not himself thought up and put into words, something for which he cannot alone assume complete responsibility.

VNA

FROM VÉRA NABOKOV LETTER TO MARIE SCHÉBÉKO,[47] MAY 28, 1960

Nous avons reçu de Gallimard un exemplaire d'INVITATION AU SUPPLICE édité avec autant de soins et dans la même belle série que LOLITA.

We have received from Gallimard a copy of INVITATION AU SUPPLICE published with as much care and in the same fine series as LOLITA.

VNA

INVITATION TO A BEHEADING

[First British (Weidenfeld and Nicolson) edition published June 3, 1960]

FROM VÉRA NABOKOV LETTER TO GILBERT AND PATRICIA KIP MILLSTEIN, JULY 2, 1960

My husband asks me to thank you for sending him the play.[48] It was forwarded to this small mountain resort[49] in the Sierras, where we do not have a copy of the book. So for the moment he wants me to tell you that he is delighted by your enthusiasm, that he likes, among a number of things, the structure of the play, the scene with little Emmie, the end (four prop men). He thinks that for the sake of "unity" it was a happy thought to combine the jailers' meal with the "last supper" scene, and for the sake of economy, to make little Emmy emerge from the opening in the wall, sharing the plot with M'sieur Pierre. He thinks you have worked with amazing speed and dexterity, and has many complimentary remarks to make. With other things he does not find himself in complete agreement. In fact, there [are] a number of changes that he would like you to make, if you will. I am writing now mainly to find out if you would agree to rework certain scenes and to introduce those changes which fall into three main categories: 1. certain stylistic improvements, 2. certain alterations in characterizations, 3. some structural changes.

Here are a few examples:

Stylistically, he finds unsatisfactory p. 1-1-7. This is not a good way to show the "puppet" or "automaton" quality of the people of the town, mainly because it is out of character for C., who is a *poet*, to use clichés, or indeed to make this kind of wasteful speeches. My husband also does not like C. to say "Do I have any choice," p. 1-2-13 (for the same reason); does not like the speech "I will tell you why I am accused" etc., p. 1-2-16, as well as the last remark on this page; and the whole second part of C.'s conversation with his mother. Incidentally, Cecilia should not use, in part, C.'s own experience for reasons given below.

Characterizations: 1) C. must be seen as a poet, a creator. This characterizes his thought, his approach to life and to his compatriots, and, of course, to his wife. My husband thinks there should be some samples of what C. thinks or writes. He has no one to talk to, but prisoners do talk to themselves. 2) Marthe. It seems at first glance a good idea to make Marthe as repulsive physically as she is spiritually (falsies). But actually, this is a blind alley. She must be attractive physically, though she may be given some one defect. It is her beauty that inspires C.'s love with a hope that somehow, somewhere, beyond the sham world they live in, some spiritual rapport may be established between them. This hope, of course, is never realized, but without an attractive shell, we do not get the particular "betrayal" realized through Marthe's person. 3) The mother. She is not one of C.'s own kind. C.'s father obviously was. There is a deliberate mystery about his identity and C.'s conception. Was his mother a victim, or was it merely the unforeseen ending of an affair between a wayward precocious girl and someone ("perhaps, a sailor") descended from Byron's Corsair, a Byronic character in a much later disguise (21st century? 22nd?) The mother's personality may have been ever so slightly tinged by the contact with that rebel, but she is timorous and feeble. Her betrayal is not in her joining with the jailers in their feast but in her going to Marthe for protection, for a certificate that she had never had any contact with her son. 3) [sic] Librarian. His "no" would be more effective if coming (as in the book) to deny M'sieur Pierre's ingenuity in guessing the card (it is the wrong card) than to refuse to choose the card. 4) Rodrig and Rodion must be almost identical. They merge. (I must go back for a moment to C.: he must be small and slender. Much more pathetic this way.) They may be quite alike seen from the back: both largish, squarish, Khrushchyov'ish. 5) The four prop men at the end must be quite human, realistic, but not resembling C. or each other: [in] the world into which C. must go, people have each his own face.

Perhaps the most important of all is the loss, in the play, of the poetical element of the book. This element is represented (in the book) by C.'s thoughts (thought and written), by the scene of his descent, his walking on air, from that window at school, by his wonderful, completely unselfish love for horrible little Marthe, and, above all, by the theme of the Tamara Gardens. These gardens are described (could this, perhaps, appear in part in C.'s letter to Marthe, which he might read to himself while resuming its writing after some interruption?), they are then seen from the tower, and finally they appear again in the scene of the banquet when their humid, mysterious depths and recesses suddenly lose all their mystery and become exposed in the tawdry illumination (colored bulbs) provided by the city fathers. This is the final and perhaps the most important "betrayal": for this represents not the exposure of a tawdry individual, or of the state, but of the very essence of the world in which C. is living and dying. Moreover, my husband thinks that this banquet scene is one of the most spectacular and should not be omitted, introductions, speeches, illumination and all. If, for reasons of unity, you wish to have the banquet scene inside the fortress, perhaps a much larger room, with a terrace in the back opening on a grand view of the gardens, could be set up inside the fortress. (The Governor's quarters?) The family should not take part (except the brothers) but the scene should be well populated. My husband would also like to have the scene of the family's visit closer to the book, Marthe on her settee etc. And he thinks that the remark about "the property" should go.

The last scene: My husband is not sure about the actual beheading. Will it not be rather "*grand Guignol*"ish? Would it not be better to have C. get up while the headman is swinging his axe, and to have Pierre and his assistants freeze in whatever pose they happen to be at the moment? And further, after the people and decor have been carted away by the four prop men, would it not be best to have a wide meadow, left empty of houses and people, with a tender sky before, and C. going toward voices of unseen creatures calling to him? C. lifts his arms and answers them "I am coming." My husband would like to know how you feel about this suggestion.

I see I forgot to mention one more of my husband's objections: He does not care for C. to say to Emmie "Out there is the city" etc. He thinks this "too utilitarian."

Now the worst (for me) is over, and I hope I have faithfully rendered my husband's remarks. He and I both hope that you will agree to consider them and will let us know what you think of them. Please keep in mind that all these are suggestions, and that my husband, in turn, will be happy to give his complete and sympathetic attention to any remarks and suggestions coming from you.

VNA

FROM WALTER MINTON LETTER TO VÉRA NABOKOV,
AUGUST 2, 1960

The fact of the matter is that we have not been as successful with INVITATION as I had reason to hope. Aside from the so-called intellectual magazines, I found that many reviewers were somewhat puzzled by the book. Then, too, there is undeniably the fact that the reissue of SEBASTIAN KNIGHT hurt us for it came a bit before INVITATION, was widely and well reviewed as indeed it should have been and was regarded as the Nabokov reissue. That means that people going into the stores may have found two books facing them and picked the one written originally in English.

VNA

FROM VÉRA NABOKOV LETTER TO WALTER MINTON,
AUGUST 7, 1960

Mrs. Millstein has submitted a revised and immeasurably improved version of the play (INVITATION), which Vladimir has approved. So please go ahead with the contract.

VNA

FROM VN LETTER TO DAVID C. MEARNS,
SEPTEMBER 27, 1960

I shall send you within a few days, by Railway Express, another batch of my papers and manuscripts. [. . .]

I am enclosing a descriptive list of the papers I am about to send.
[. . .]

_____

Material given to The Library of Congress on Sept. 28, 1960
[. . .]
4. Corrected typescript and set of galley proofs of INVITATION TO A BEHEADING, publ. by Putnam, 1959 (transl. by Dmitri Nabokov, corrections by V. Nabokov).
5. 4 pages of proof of French translation, corrected by V. Nabokov (trans. by Jarl Priel), of Foreword written in English for the Putnam edition of INVITATION TO A BEHEADING.

Library of Congress, Nabokov Correspondence file

FROM VN LETTER TO GERMANO FACETTI,[50]
APRIL 13, 1963

I think a cover should have some aesthetic appeal. Mr. André Francois' macrocephalic homunculus has none. Moreover, I object to the style he has chosen with its, by now academic, simplifications and distortions. I am returning your sketch and am sending you another one. It is in the spirit of the book and translates some of its poetical quality (which is absent from the pseudochildish drawing you sent me). I would be happy if you could use it as is. If there exists some technical reason against using it, then at least you will have a clear idea of what I want for this book.

VNA

FROM VN LETTER TO PENGUIN BOOKS, AUGUST 3, 1963

I have not yet received my copies of your edition of INVITATION TO A BEHEADING, but my son, who received two copies from the Art Department, has shown the book to me. I am absolutely delighted with its appearance. Thank you very much.

I think my son, who made the sketch for the cover, should be now paid for it.

His name, incidentally, is Dmitri Nabokov (not Dmitry).

VNA

FROM VÉRA NABOKOV LETTER TO WALTER MINTON, SEPTEMBER 15, 1963

Two Danish composers (each of them acting separately) want to put the book to music, one as an opera, the other as a TV opera.

VNA

FROM ROBERT SHANKLAND[51] LETTER TO VN, DECEMBER 7, 1965

The Radio Liberty Committee is deeply interested in re-publishing new Russian-language editions of some or all of those early works of yours that you wrote in Russian. The editions would probably be printed in Paris and would definitely appear without Radio Liberty attribution, either in the editions themselves or in any accompanying promotion.

VNA

FROM VÉRA NABOKOV LETTER TO ROBERT SHANKLAND, MARCH 4, 1966

My husband agrees that INVITATION TO A BEHEADING is a very good choice.[52]

FROM ROBERT SHANKLAND LETTER TO VÉRA NABOKOV, APRIL 5, 1966

No copies[53] will be for sale (although for tactical reasons, a price will be shown on the book). Except for a few scattered copies (gifts to you, etc.) the entire edition will be circulated inside the Soviet Union. [. . .]

As I noted early in our correspondence, this is an experimental project. We expect in 1966 to produce four books: your husband's, plus translations of Camus's *L'Étranger* and Joyce's *Dubliners* and *Portrait*.

VNA

FROM ROBERT SHANKLAND LETTER TO VÉRA NABOKOV, MAY 24, 1966

[. . .] we will probably have the new edition of *Priglashenie na kazn'* printed by Berezniak in Paris. [. . .] He did the Camus book, of which I sent you a copy on May 16. The publisher, as with that book, would be Editions Victor, Paris.

VNA

FROM VÉRA NABOKOV LETTER TO MORRILL CODY,[54] JULY 9, 1966

Unfortunately, the misprints are so numerous that my husband finds he must see the final proofs. [. . .]
In order to avoid new misprints, my husband reluctantly accepts the substitution of dots for dashes, and dashes for inverted commas, although this substitution is unfortunate in view of the fact that dots, dashes and inverted commas all had their carefully assigned meaning in the original.

VNA

FROM VÉRA NABOKOV LETTER TO ROBERT SHANKLAND, JULY 20, 1966

He has a rule never to argue with critics writing about him, never to express either gratitude or objections regarding their literary opinions. But he wonders if in the present case[55] it is not a kind of duty for him to set right some factual errors.
[. . .] Even more incongruous in my husband's opinion is the parallel that Mr. M. establishes (p. 7) between Cincinnatus C. [. . .]

and the protagonist of the Dostoevsky story inaccurately named by the American translators Memoirs (or is it Diary) from the Underground; Cincinnatus, the only positive character in the novel, a poet and a thinker, has nothing whatever in common with the deliberately contemptible hero of the UNDERGROUND who is meant by Dostoevski to be a vicious, narrowminded and essentially pedestrian character. [. . .]

Since Mr. Moynahan's article is otherwise most sensitive and intelligent, and my husband would by no means wish to offend him, my husband wishes to leave it to you.

VNA

INTERVIEW WITH ALFRED APPEL, JR., SEPTEMBER 25–29, 1966[56]

Generally speaking, I am a slow writer, a snail carrying its house at the rate of two hundred pages of final copy per year (one spectacular exception was the Russian original of *Invitation to a Beheading*, the first draft of which I wrote in one fortnight of wonderful excitement and sustained inspiration).

SO, 68

. . . *do you have one novel towards which you feel the most affection, which you esteem over all others?*

The most affection, *Lolita*; the greatest esteem, *Priglashenie na Kazn'*.

SO, 92

FROM VN LETTER TO ANDREW FIELD,[57] SEPTEMBER 29, 1966

p. 266 both my wife and I regret that you do not appreciate the poetry of *Priglashenie na kazn'*. It is the only prose poem I have composed. But of course I am not challenging your views.

VNA

FROM VÉRA NABOKOV LETTER TO MORRILL CODY,
NOVEMBER 25, 1966

We received two copies of your beautiful INVITATION TO A
BEHEADING in its delightful orange-and-purple jacket. My husband asks me to thank you. He is especially grateful for the loving
care you took of this edition and is very happy to have it in print
again.

VNA

FROM MORRILL CODY LETTER TO VÉRA NABOKOV,
NOVEMBER 29, 1966

[. . .] we are mailing some four hundred copies to our correspon-
dents in the Soviet Union and hundreds of others will find their way
up there with travelers and in response to requests.

VNA

FROM VÉRA NABOKOV LETTER TO WALTER MINTON,
SEPTEMBER 29, 1968

Mr. McGrath's adaptation for the stage of Vladimir's INVITA-
TION TO A BEHEADING is definitely to be produced by the
Shakespeare Festival Theatre of New York.
[. . .]

VNA

INTERVIEW WITH ALDEN WHITMAN, APRIL 1969[58]

11. Why have you chosen, in many stories, to create characters
preoccupied with their pasts, often touched off by a death?
11. My creatures are not more preoccupied with the past than any
other novelist's creatures. Most of mine (I say most because, for
instance, the man in *Invitation to a Beheading* triumphantly transcends the scaffold) must die some day one way or another.

VNA

INTERVIEW WITH ALLENE TALMEY, LATE 1969[59]

You have witnessed extraordinary changes in your lifetime and maintained an "esthetic distance." Would you consider this a matter of your temperament or a quality you had to cultivate?

My aloofness is an illusion resulting from my never having belonged to any literary, political, or social coterie. I am a lone lamb. Let me submit, however, that I have bridged the "esthetic distance" in my own way by means of such absolutely final indictments of Russian and German totalitarianism as my novels *Invitation to a Beheading* and *Bend Sinister*.

SO, 156

ANNIVERSARY NOTES, WRITTEN MARCH 10, 1970[60]

On Robert Alter: Mr. Alter's essay on the "Art of Politics in *Invitation to a Beheading*" is a most brilliant reflection of that book in a reader's mind. It is practically flawless so that all I can add is that I particularly appreciated his citing a passage from *The Gift* "that could serve as a useful gloss on the entire nature of political and social reality in the earlier novel."

On Stanley Edgar Hyman: Mr. Hyman in his first-rate piece "The Handle" discusses *Invitation to a Beheading* and *Bend Sinister*, the two bookends of grotesque design between which my other volumes tightly huddle. [. . .]

On Robert P. Hughes: Mr. Hughes in his "Notes on the Translation of *Invitation to a Beheading*" is one of the few critics who noticed the poetry of the Tamara terraces with their metamorphosed tamaracks. In the trance of objectivity which the reading of the festschrift has now induced in me, I am able to say that Mr. Hughes' discussion of the trials and triumphs attending that translation is very subtle and rewarding.

SO, 287, 295–96

FROM LETTER FROM NIKOLAY ANDREEV TO VN, JULY 25, 1971

[Andreev passes on a letter he received in early July 1971 from an unnamed Anglo-Russian friend living in Moscow]

Nabokov's books have reached us. He is, I would say, definitely one of the most popular authors of the day in discerning circles in Moscow. "Dar" is read and re-read. . . . Everyone who has read our copy has been particularly struck and most unholily delighted by the chapter on Chernyshevsky. *Priglashenie na kazn'* awakes violent and various reactions. One friend of ours who spent seventeen years in camps and now works as a vice-director of a museum says that it is a book about himself and that the Rodion figure is a true portrait of his immediate boss. Others are irritated – artificial, like a coloured film. Others find the artificiality entrancing.

VNA

FROM JOAN DALY[61] LETTER TO VÉRA NABOKOV, JUNE 12, 1972

[Approves licensing James Osbourne's new adaptation of *Invitation to a Beheading* for Theatre 3 in Edmonton]

VNA

FROM VÉRA NABOKOV LETTER TO WALTER MINTON, JUNE 17, 1972

The Czechs cannot export the money, and did not publish.[62]

FROM VÉRA NABOKOV LETTER TO ANTOINE GALLIMARD,[63] OCTOBER 10, 1979

[They are wrong] qualifier ce roman d'une "caricature désesperée," étant donné la fin plutôt optimiste.

[. . .] to call this novel a "despairing caricature," in view of its rather optimistic ending.

VNA

NOTES

1. *Speak, Memory: An Autobiography Revisited* (New York: G. P. Putnam's Sons, 1966), 279.

2. Letter to Edmund Wilson, December 15, 1940, *Nabokov-Wilson Letters*, ed. Simon Karlinsky (New York: Harper and Row, 1979), 33 (hereafter, *NWL*). See also *Speak, Memory*, 278–79; and *Drugie berega* (New York: Chekhov, 1954), 238.

3. *Daily Dispatch and Manchester Morning Chronicle*, March 31, 1922, 6; see Brian Boyd, *Vladimir Nabokov: The Russian Years* (Princeton, N.J.: Princeton University Press, 1990), 34.

4.

"Роман, который теперь пишу--после 'Отчаяния'--чудовищно трудно; между прочим, герой мой работает над биографией Чернышевского, поэтому мне пришлось прочесть те многочисленные книги, которые об этом господине написаны--и всё это по своему переварить, и теперь у меня изжога. Он был бездарнее многих, но многим мужественнее. "

("The novel I'm writing now – after 'Despair' – is monstrously hard; among other things, my hero works on a biography of Chernyshevsky, so I have had to read through the numerous books written about this gent – and digest all this in my own way, and now I have heartburn. He was more talentless than many, but braver than many.") (Berberova Collection, Beinecke Library, Yale)

5. *Strong Opinions* (New York: McGraw-Hill, 1973), 68 (see above).

6. Vladimir Nabokov Archive, Berg Collection, New York Public Library (hereafter, VNA).

7. For other connections between the two novels, see Boyd, *Vladimir Nabokov: The Russian Years*, 416–17.

8. Letter to Andrew Field, September 26, 1966, VNA (see above).

9. Translated by Dmitri Nabokov and Michael Scammell in collaboration with VN (New York: G. P. Putnam's Sons, 1963).

10. For a reproduction of this manuscript page, see Boyd, *Vladimir Nabokov: The Russian Years*, 446j.

11. Nabokov's mother.

12. Writer and friend, living at this time in Brussels.

13. Of the Paris-based émigré journal *Sovremennye zapiski*.

14. Cf. Gennady Barabtarlo, "Nabokov Papers in the University of Illinois (Urbana-Champaign) Archives," *The Nabokovian* 28 (1992): 66–74; see pp. 69–70.

15. Anna Lazarevna Feigin, Véra Nabokov's cousin, with whom the Nabokovs were living at 22 Nestorstrasse, Berlin.

16. Noted as going on sale on this date in *Poslednie novosti*, June 22, 1935.

17. Noted as going on sale on this date in *Poslednie novosti*, November 17, 1935.

18. Noted as going on sale on this date in *Poslednie novosti*, February 27, 1936.

19. A Swedish translator.

20. Emigré publishing house in Paris.

21. Of *Sovremennye zapiski*.

22. The question of its publication in book form.

23. One of the editors of *Sovremennye zapiski*, which sometimes acted as a publisher of books (such as Nabokov's *Podvig* [*Glory*] in 1932).

24. Nabokov's American literary agent.

25. From Véra Nabokov's transcript of the original.

26. Paris émigré newspaper.

27. Paris émigré newspaper.

28. Evgeny Sablin, former Russian chargé d'affaires.

29. Writer, critic, and new friend.

30. Head of New Directions.

31. Published *Partisan Review*, January–February 1951, and as chapter 14 of *Conclusive Evidence* (New York: Harper and Brothers, 1951), revised as *Speak, Memory* (1966).

32. Of Clairouin, Nabokov's literary agent in Europe.

33. Russian-born, French-educated Greek consul in Tunis who had translated *Priglashenie na kazn'* into French in 1943 to keep himself busy.

34. *Lolita* had begun to cause a sensation in France, after the French government had banned it in December 1956 along with other English-language books published by Olympia Press, Paris.

35. Marcelle Sibon had translated Nabokov's *Nikolai Gogol* into French for La Table Ronde (1953).

36. Of Gallimard.

37. Mohrt replied on April 23 that *he* had not seen Priel's translation and, on reading it, now found it good.

38. Head of G. P. Putnam's Sons.

39. Manuscript Division, Library of Congress.

40. Misdated "1958."

41. Cofounder of Weidenfeld and Nicolson.

42. *Selected Letters 1940–1977*, ed. Dmitri Nabokov and Matthew Bruccoli (New York: Harcourt Brace Jovanovich / Bruccoli, Clark, Layman, 1989).

43. Misdated "1958."

44. Of *Lolita*.

45. Written from Sedona, Arizona.

46. Of the Committee Against Capital Punishment, California.

47. Of Clairouin, Nabokov's literary agent in Europe.

48. Patricia Kip Millstein had adapted *Invitation to Beheading* for the stage, with the help of her husband Gilbert, of the *New York Times*.

49. Big Pine, California.

50. Of Penguin Books.

51. Of Radio Liberty Committee, Munich, a CIA affiliate.

52. On December 20, 1965, she had written to Robert Shankland listing VN's preferred sequence as the Russian *Lolita*, *Dar*, and *Priglashenie na kazn'*; on February 25, 1966, Shankland replied that the vote was for *Priglashenie na kazn'*.

53. Of the edition of 2,000.

54. Of Radio Liberty.

55. Julian Moynahan had been asked to write a preface for the Editions Victor reprint.

56. "An Interview with Vladimir Nabokov," *Wisconsin Studies in Contemporary Literature* 8.2 (Spring 1967): 127–52; rpt., *SO*.

57. In response to the manuscript of Field's *Nabokov: His Life in Art* (Boston: Little, Brown, 1967).

58. From typescript; not in the interview as published, "Nabokov, Nearing 70, Describes His 'New Girl,'" *New York Times*, April 19, 1969, or in the version printed in *SO*.

59. "Vladimir Nabokov Talks about Vladimir Nabokov," *Vogue* (December 1969): 190–91.

60. Published as a supplement to the Winter 1970 issue of *TriQuarterly*; rpt., *SO*.

61. Of Paul, Weiss, Rifkind, Wharton, and Garrison, VN's New York lawyers.

62. During the "Prague Spring," the Czechs had been given the rights to publish their own edition of *Invitation to a Beheading*, but publication was stopped by the Soviet invasion of August 1968.

63. Of Gallimard.

IV SELECT BIBLIOGRAPHY

Select Bibliography

This bibliography does not attempt to provide a comprehensive guide to scholarship on Vladimir Nabokov. In the main, it includes individual articles devoted to *Invitation to a Beheading*, broader studies of Nabokov that devote significant attention to the novel, and works that provide useful information on Nabokov's biography.

Alexandrov, Vladimir E. *Nabokov's Otherworld*. Princeton, N.J.: Princeton University Press, 1991.

   A detailed analysis of the manner in which Nabokov's metaphysics inform and shape the ethical and aesthetic dimensions of his work.

Alexandrov, Vladimir E., ed. *The Garland Companion to Vladimir Nabokov*. Garland Reference Library of the Humanities 1474. New York: Garland, 1995.

   An invaluable collection of articles on a wide variety of topics, from Nabokov's poetry to his reception by literary critics; the volume includes individual essays on each of Nabokov's novels, as well as essays dealing with Nabokov's artistic relationship to a host of other writers.

Alter, Robert. "*Invitation to a Beheading*: Nabokov and the Art of Politics." *TriQuarterly* 17 (1970): 41–59. Reprinted in Appel, Jr., and Newman, *Nabokov*, 41–59 (see below).

   Alter's insightful discussion elucidates the political ramifications of Nabokov's vision of art and aesthetics in the novel.

Appel, Alfred, Jr., and Charles Newman, eds. *Nabokov: Criticism, Reminiscences, Translations and Tributes*. Evanston, Ill.: Northwestern University Press, 1971.

   This collection contains essays on Nabokov's life and work, commentary on his achievements as a translator, and a series of short appreciations by numerous writers and critics.

Barabtarlo, Gennady. *Aerial View: Essays on Nabokov's Art and Metaphysics*. American University Studies. Series 24, American Literature, Vol. 40. New York: Peter Lang, 1993.

Barabtarlo's collection of brief essays includes a revised version of the article on *Invitation to a Beheading* that appeared in the *Slavic Review* (see below), as well as a note decoding the enigmatic phrase "*Mali è trano t'amesti*," which is sung by Marthe's brother in Cincinnatus's cell.

———. "Within and Without Cincinnatus's Cell: Reference Gauges in Nabokov's *Invitation to a Beheading*." *Slavic Review* 49.3 (1990): 390–97.

Barabtarlo focuses on the significance of the pencil and the spider in Cincinnatus's spiritual evolution.

Berdjis, Nassim Winnie. *Imagery in Vladimir Nabokov's Last Russian Novel (Dar), Its English Translation (The Gift), and Other Prose Works of the 1930s.* Mainzer Studien zur Amerikanistik 31. Frankfurt: Peter Lang, 1995.

An extensive study of recurring images and thematic patterns in Nabokov's prose of the 1930s.

Bitsilli, P. M. "The Revival of Allegory." Translated by Dwight Stephens. *TriQuarterly* 17 (1970): 102–18. Reprinted in Appel, Jr., and Newman, *Nabokov*, 102–18.

Bitsilli takes the position that Nabokov's work is "allegorical" and that Cincinnatus is an "everyman"; he compares Nabokov's artistic methods with those of Nikolay Gogol and Mikhail Saltykov-Shchedrin.

———. "V. Nabokov's *Invitation to a Beheading* and *The Eye*." Translated by D. Barton Johnson. In Proffer, *A Book of Things*, 65–69 (see below). Reprinted in Page, *Nabokov*, 56–60. (The original review appeared in *Sovremennye zapiski* 68 [1939]: 474–77.)

Bitsilli discusses the sound texture and metaphors of Nabokov's novel, and he argues that Cincinnatus and Pierre are two aspects of "man in general."

———. "Vozrozhdenie allegorii." *Sovremennye zapiski* 61 (1936): 191–204.

The original text of "The Revival of Allegory."

Blackwell, Stephen. "Reading and Rupture in Nabokov's *Invitation to a Beheading*." *Slavic and East European Journal* 39.1 (1994): 38–53.

Blackwell analyzes the transformative effect that reading has both on Cincinnatus and on the reader of Nabokov's novel.

Bloom, Harold, ed. *Vladimir Nabokov*. Modern Critical Views. New York: Chelsea House, 1987.

A collection of essays devoted to various aspects of Nabokov's art, particularly his English-language fiction.

Boegeman, Margaret Byrd. "*Invitation to a Beheading* and the Many Shades of Kafka." In Rivers and Nicol, *Nabokov's Fifth Arc*, 105–21 (see below).

Boegeman identifies parallels between Nabokov's novel and Kafka's fiction, and she argues that *Invitation to a Beheading* expresses the writer's concern over his intention to switch from Russian to English in his literary work.

Boyd, Brian. *Vladimir Nabokov: The American Years*. Princeton, N.J.: Princeton University Press, 1991.

———. *Vladimir Nabokov: The Russian Years*. Princeton: Princeton University Press, 1990.

Boyd's detailed account of Nabokov's life and literary career provides a wealth of information on the writer's biography as well as thoughtful readings of his major and minor works.

Buks, Nora. "Eshafot v khrustal'nom dvortse: o romane Vl. Nabokova *Priglashenie na kazn'.*" *Cahiers du Monde russe* 35.4 (1994): 821–38.

This article explores in detail the relationship between *Invitation to a Beheading* and *The Gift*.

Clancy, Laurie. *The Novels of Vladimir Nabokov*. New York: St. Martin's, 1984.

Clancy's survey of Nabokov's long fiction treats *Invitation to a Beheading* primarily as a "political parable."

Connolly, Julian. *Nabokov's Early Fiction: Patterns of Self and Other*. Cambridge: Cambridge University Press, 1992.

This study of the work that Nabokov originally wrote in Russian analyzes Nabokov's evolving approach to the depiction of the relationship between one character and another, between character and author, and between author and reader.

———. "Nabokov's 'Terra Incognita' and 'Invitation to a Beheading': The Struggle for Imaginative Freedom." *Wiener Slawistischer Almanach* 12 (1983): 55–65.

This article discusses the affinities and differences between one of Nabokov's short stories and *Invitation to a Beheading*.

Cooke, Brett, and Alexander Grinyakin. "Nabokov on the Moscow Stage." *The Nabokovian* 25 (1990): 22–25.

Contains a brief account of a Moscow stage adaptation of *Invitation to a Beheading*.

Couturier, Maurice, ed. *Nabokov: Autobiography, Biography and Fiction.* Special issue of *Cycnos* 10.1 (1993).

This collection of papers delivered at a conference devoted to Nabokov contains Leona Toker's article on Nabokov's treatment of totalitarianism in *Invitation to a Beheading* and *Bend Sinister*.

————. *Nabokov: At the Crossroads of Modernism and Postmodernism.* Special issue of *Cycnos* 12.2 (1995).

The essays published in this collection derive from the proceedings of a conference broadly concerned with Nabokov's relationship to modernist and postmodernist currents in literature.

Davydov, Sergej. "*Invitation to a Beheading.*" In Vladimir E. Alexandrov, ed., *The Garland Companion to Vladimir Nabokov,* 188–203. New York: Garland, 1995.

Davydov's essay highlights the Gnostic elements of the novel.

————. "*Teksty-Matreški*" *Vladimira Nabokova.* Munich: Otto Sagner, 1982.

In this study of selected Nabokov works, Davydov explores in more detail the Gnostic elements discussed in his essay on *Invitation to a Beheading* in *The Garland Companion to Vladimir Nabokov.*

Dembo, L. S., ed. *Nabokov: The Man and His Work.* Madison: University of Wisconsin Press, 1967.

This anthology contains essays on Nabokov's work, an interview with the author, and a bibliography of articles and reviews of his work.

Dolinin, A[leksandr]. "*Priglashenie na kazn'.*" In *Vladimir Nabokov: Rasskazy. Priglashenie na kazn'. Roman. Esse, interv'iu, retsenzii,* 503–10. Moscow: Kniga, 1989.

Dolinin's notes to a Russian edition of the novel provide a concise review of the early critical responses to the work.

Field, Andrew. *Nabokov: His Life in Art.* Boston: Little, Brown, 1967.

This early monograph on Nabokov offered insight into those parts of Nabokov's *oeuvre* that had not been translated into English and therefore were unavailable to readers without a knowledge of Russian.

Foster, John Burt, Jr. *Nabokov's Art of Memory and European Modernism.* Princeton, N.J.: Princeton University Press, 1993.

Foster's study of Nabokov's relationship to the modernist tradition focuses on the evolution of Nabokov's treatment of memory.

Foster, Ludmila A. "Nabokov's Gnostic Turpitude: The Surrealistic Vision of Reality in *Priglašenie na kazn'*." In Joachim T. Baer and Norman W. Ingham, eds., *Mnemozina: Studia litteraria russica in honorem Vsevolod Setchkarev*, 117–29. Munich: Wilhelm Fink, 1974.

Foster explores the surrealistic qualities of Nabokov's novel, which she finds to be ruled by the logic of dreams.

Galtseva, Renata, and Irina Rodnyanskaya. "The Obstacle: The Human Being, or the Twentieth Century in the Mirror of Dystopia." In Thomas Lahusen, ed., *Perestroika: Perspectives on Modernization*. Special issue of *South Atlantic Quarterly* 90.2 (1991): 293–322.

This analysis of twentieth-century dystopian fiction discusses *Invitation to a Beheading* along with works by Zamiatin, Kafka, Platonov, Orwell, and Huxley.

Gibian, George, and Stephen Jan Parker, eds. *The Achievements of Vladimir Nabokov: Essays, Studies, Reminiscences, and Stories*. Ithaca, N.Y.: Center for International Studies, 1984.

This anthology of papers about Nabokov's life and work includes an article in which Slava Paperno and John V. Hagopian outline "official" and "unofficial" responses to Nabokov's work in the Soviet Union.

Grayson, Jane. *Nabokov Translated: A Comparison of Nabokov's Russian and English Prose*. Oxford: Oxford University Press, 1977.

A pioneering study of the changes and revisions Nabokov introduced into the translations of his work.

Grossmith, Robert. "Spiralizing the Circle: The Gnostic Subtext in Nabokov's *Invitation to a Beheading*." *Essays in Poetics* 12.2 (1987): 51–74.

Grossmith's analysis of Gnostic and Neoplatonic elements in *Invitation to a Beheading* devotes particular attention to images of circularity and asymmetry in the novel.

Houk, Guy. "The Spider and the Moth: Nabokov's *Priglašenie na kazn'* as Epistemological Exhortation." *Russian Literature* 18 (1985): 31–41.

Houk traces Cincinnatus's efforts to overcome his fear and to allow his imagination to triumph over tyranny.

Hughes, Robert P. "Notes on the Translation of *Invitation to a Beheading*." *TriQuarterly* 17 (1970): 284–92. Rpt. in Appel, Jr., and Newman, *Nabokov*, 284–92.

Hughes examines several of the specific linguistic and semantic changes Nabokov and his son made when translating the novel into English.

Hyde, G. M. *Vladimir Nabokov: America's Russian Novelist*. Critical Appraisals Series. London: Marion Boyars, 1977.

In his survey of Nabokov's novels, Hyde comments on several of the main themes of *Invitation to a Beheading* and compares the novel to *Bend Sinister*.

Hyman, Stanley Edgar. "The Handle: *Invitation to a Beheading* and *Bend Sinister*." *TriQuarterly* 17 (1970): 60–71. Rpt. in Appel, Jr., and Newman, *Nabokov*, 60–71.

Hyman's article looks at Nabokov's handling of character and finds that Krug, the protagonist of *Bend Sinister*, is a more vulnerable figure than Cincinnatus because of his attachment to the things of his world, especially his son.

Johnson, D. Barton. *Worlds in Regression: Some Novels of Vladimir Nabokov*. Ann Arbor: Ardis, 1985.

This collection contains a dozen essays dealing with various aspects of Nabokov's art (from chess to chromesthesia); two of these essays concentrate on the art and metaphysics of *Invitation to a Beheading*.

Juliar, Michael. *Vladimir Nabokov: A Descriptive Bibliography*. Garland Reference Library of the Humanities 656. New York: Garland, 1986.

Juliar's bibliography includes publication information on the entire spectrum of Nabokov's work – fiction, poetry, plays, translations, recordings, interviews, drawings, and so on.

Karlinsky, Simon, ed. *The Nabokov-Wilson Letters. Correspondence Between Vladimir Nabokov and Edmund Wilson, 1940–1971*. New York: Harper Colophon, 1980.

Nabokov and Wilson engage in a spirited debate about a wide range of subjects, with a particular emphasis on literary interpretation and translation.

Khodasevich, Vladislav. "On Sirin." Edited by Simon Karlinsky and Robert P. Hughes. Translated by Michael H. Walker. *TriQuarterly* 17 (1970): 96–101. Rpt. in Appel, Jr., and Newman, *Nabokov*, 96–101.

Khodasevich's pioneering article argues that the central subject of Nabokov's fiction is art and that his protagonists must be understood primarily as representations of aspiring artists.

———. "O Sirine." *Vozrozhdenie* 13 February 1937: 9.

The original text of the excerpt translated by Michael Walker with the title "On Sirin."

Kopper, John M. "The Prison in Nabokov's *Priglašenie*: A Place to Have the Time of One's Life." *Russian Language Journal* 41, no. 140 (1987): 175–84.

Taking the theme of time as his departure point, Kopper explores Nabokov's novel as a paradigmatic work of modernism.

Klemtner, Susan Strehle. "To 'Special Space': Transformotion in *Invitation to a Beheading*." In Charles S. Ross, ed., *Vladimir Nabokov*. Special issue of *Modern Fiction Studies* 25.3 (1979): 427–38.

Klemtner focuses on the themes of movement and stasis in the novel.

Lee, L[awrence] L. *Vladimir Nabokov*. Twayne's United States Authors Series 266. Boston: Twayne, 1976.

This monograph contains a short biography of Nabokov, a broad survey of his career (concentrating on the major themes of the prose fiction), and a brief annnotated bibliography.

Moynahan, Julian. "A Russian Preface for Nabokov's *Beheading*." *Novel* 1 (1967): 12–18.

In this brief introduction to the novel, Moynahan touches on the Gnostic resonance he detects in it, and he speaks of Nabokov's relationship to the Russian and Western literary traditions.

Nabokov, Vladimir. *Lectures on Literature*. Edited by Fredson Bowers. New York: Harcourt Brace Jovanovich / Bruccoli Clark, 1980.

This collection of notes that Nabokov used as the basis for class lectures contains two important pieces, "Good Readers and Good Writers" and "The Art of Literature and Commonsense."

———. *Lectures on Russian Literature*. Edited by Fredson Bowers. New York: Harcourt Brace Jovanovich / Bruccoli Clark, 1981.

This volume contains Nabokov's lecture notes on such writers as Gogol, Dostoevsky, and Tolstoy.

———. *Selected Letters, 1940–1977*. Edited by Dmitri Nabokov and Matthew J. Bruccoli. New York: Harcourt Brace Jovanovich / Bruccoli Clark Layman, 1989.

This collection of some four hundred letters to publishers, scholars, and family members provides a glimpse into Nabokov's far-reaching activities, from lepidoptery to literature.

———. *Speak, Memory. An Autobiography Revisited.* New York: G. P. Putnam's Sons, 1966.

Nabokov's finely crafted and highly poetic autobiography concentrates on his childhood and youth.

———. *Strong Opinions.* New York: McGraw-Hill, 1973.

A collection of interviews and short essays prepared and edited by Nabokov.

Oles, Brian Thomas. "Silence and the Ineffable in Nabokov's *Invitation to a Beheading.*" *Nabokov Studies* 2 (1995): 191–212.

An exploration of the importance of silence, both actual and aesthetic, in Nabokov's work.

Page, Norman, ed. *Nabokov: The Critical Heritage.* The Critical Heritage Series. London: Routledge and Kegan Paul, 1982.

A collection of reviews of Nabokov's works, including four brief reviews of the English-language edition of *Invitation to a Beheading.*

Parker, Stephen Jan. *Understanding Vladimir Nabokov.* Columbia: University of South Carolina Press, 1987.

A concise introduction to Nabokov's art, particularly his major fiction; includes a brief annotated bibliography.

Penner, Dick. "*Invitation to a Beheading*: Nabokov's Absurdist Initiation." *Critique: Studies in Modern Fiction* 20.3 (1979): 27–39.

Penner argues that the novel is a classic work of absurdist literature: the absurd events in the novel ultimately lead Cincinnatus to a full awarenss of his own being.

Peterson, Dale. "Nabokov's *Invitation*: Literature as Execution." *PMLA* 96.5 (1981): 824–36. Rpt. in Bloom, *Vladimir Nabokov,* 83–99.

Peterson's engaging treatment of the novel focuses on Cincinnatus's status as a literary character subject to the predatory attention of the voracious reader.

Pifer, Ellen. *Nabokov and the Novel.* Cambridge, Mass.: Harvard University Press, 1980.

In this exploration of Nabokov's idiosyncratic approach to the depiction of life in fiction, Pifer argues that art for Nabokov does not represent a retreat from reality but rather a means of engaging reality.

Proffer, Carl R., ed. *A Book of Things about Vladimir Nabokov*. Ann Arbor, Mich.: Ardis, 1974.

Although primarily devoted to Nabokov's English-language fiction, this collection contains Bitsilli's review of *Invitation to a Beheading* and an article on Nabokov's reception by émigré critics.

Rampton, David. *Vladimir Nabokov*. Modern Novelists. New York: St. Martin's, 1993.

A succinct introduction to the artistic themes and stylistic devices found in Nabokov's major fiction.

———. *Vladimir Nabokov: A Critical Study of the Novels*. Cambridge Studies in Russian Literature. Cambridge: Cambridge University Press, 1984.

Rampton's investigation of several of Nabokov's novels interrogates the assumptions that the critic finds embedded within the works.

Rivers, J. E., and Charles Nicol, eds. *Nabokov's Fifth Arc: Nabokov and Others on His Life's Work*. Austin: University of Texas Press, 1982.

This collection of original essays and reminiscences contains Margeret Byrd Boegeman's article on Nabokov and Kafka.

Ross, Charles S., ed. *Vladimir Nabokov*. Special issue of *Modern Fiction Studies* 25.3 (1979).

A collection of articles and essays, with a "checklist" of Nabokov criticism compiled by Samuel Schuman.

Roth, Phyllis A., ed. *Critical Essays on Vladimir Nabokov*. Critical Essays on American Literature. Boston: G. K. Hall, 1984.

This collection of essays includes a detailed introduction in which Phyllis Roth chronicles the expansion and evolution of Nabokov criticism, and an annotated bibliography of major critical works compiled by Beverly Lyon Clark.

Rowe, W[illiam] W[oodin]. *Nabokov's Spectral Dimension*. Ann Arbor, Mich.: Ardis, 1981.

Rowe's investigation of Nabokov's fiction places extraordinary emphasis on the detection of ghostly forces at work behind the scenes.

Schuman, Samuel. *Vladimir Nabokov: A Reference Guide*. Boston: G. K. Hall, 1979.

Schuman's bibliography of works about Nabokov provides informative summaries of each entry's contents.

Shapiro, Gavriel. "Khristianskie motivy, ikh ikonografiia i simvolika, v romane Vladimira Nabokova 'Priglashenie na kazn'.'" *Russian Language Journal* 33, no. 116 (1979): 144–62.

A study of the religious imagery and motifs in *Invitation to a Beheading*.

———. "Konflikt mezhdu protagonistom i okruzhaiushchim ego mirom v povesti N. V. Gogolia 'Shinel'' i v romane V. V. Nabokova *Priglashenie na kazn'*." *Russian Language Journal* 34, no. 119 (1980): 109–19.

Shapiro delineates several parallel's between Gogol's short story "The Overcoat" and Nabokov's *Invitation to a Beheading*.

———. "Reministsentsii iz 'Mertvykh dush' v 'Priglashenii na kazn'' Nabokova." In S. A. Goncharov, ed., 175–81. *Gogolevskii sbornik*. St. Petersburg: Obrazovanie, 1994.

Commentary on specific parallels between Nabokov's treatment of character and setting in *Invitation to a Beheading* and Gogol's *Dead Souls*.

———. "Russkie literaturnye alliuzii v romane Nabokova *Priglashenie na kazn'*." *Russian Literature* 9 (1981): 369–78.

This article explores the resonance of several works of Russian literature in *Invitation to a Beheading*.

Stuart, Dabney. *Nabokov: The Dimensions of Parody*. Baton Rouge: Louisiana State University Press, 1978.

In his study of the distinctive organizing principles of several of Nabokov's novels, Stuart draws attention to the highly theatrical nature of the world depicted in *Invitation to a Beheading*.

Struve, Gleb. "Notes on Nabokov as a Russian Writer." In Dembo, *Nabokov*, 45–56.

One of the foremost scholars of Russian émigré literature surveys the fiction Nabokov originally wrote in Russian and comes to a conclusion often found among Nabokov's émigré critics that a supposed "lack of sympathy" for human beings in Nabokov's work was a sign that he was "alien" to the Russian literary tradition.

Tammi, Pekka. "Invitation to a Decoding. Dostoevskij as Subtext in Nabokov's *Priglašenie na kazn'*." *Scando-Slavica* 32 (1986): 51–72.

Tammi interprets the significance of parallels he finds between Nabokov's novel and Dostoevsky's *Crime and Punishment*.

———. *Problems of Nabokov's Poetics: A Narratological Analysis*. Suomalaisen

Tiedeakatemian Toimituksia Annales Academiae Scientiarum Fennicae B 231. Helsinki: Suomalainen Tiedeakatemia, 1985.

A groundbreaking analysis of Nabokov's narrational strategies.

Toker, Leona. *Nabokov: The Mystery of Literary Structures*. Ithaca, N.Y.: Cornell University Press, 1989.

Toker's sensitive reading of Nabokov's fiction reveals how minor images and motifs can carry exceptional thematic significance.

———. "'Who was becoming seasick? Cincinnatus': Some Aspects of Nabokov's Treatment of the Communist Regime." In Maurice Couturier, ed., *Nabokov: Autobiography, Biography and Fiction*. Special Issue of *Cycnos* 10.1 (1993): 81–90.

Toker compares Nabokov's treatment of totalitarian oppression in *Invitation to a Beheading* and *Bend Sinister* with works devoted to the Gulag experience.

Varshavskii, V. S. *Nezamechennoe pokolenie*. New York: Chekhov, 1956.

The section of this book devoted to *Invitation to a Beheading* highlights the political and social implications of the work.

Wood, Michael. *The Magician's Doubts: Nabokov and the Risks of Fiction*. Princeton, N.J.: Princeton University Press, 1995.

In an engaging attempt to probe behind the mask (or masks) that Nabokov presents to the reading public, Wood explores the tension he perceives between a confident, self-assured authorial persona and a more vulnerable figure who can be sensed at certain moments in Nabokov's literary texts.

Contributors

Vladimir E. Alexandrov is Professor of Russian Literature at Yale University.

Robert Alter is Class of 1937 Professor of Hebrew and Comparative Literature at the University of California at Berkeley.

Brian Boyd is Associate Professor of English at the University of Auckland.

Julian W. Connolly is Professor of Slavic Languages and Literatures at the University of Virginia.

D. Barton Johnson is Professor of Russian (emeritus) at the University of California at Santa Barbara.

Dale E. Peterson is Professor of Russian and English at Amherst College.